The Physical, the Natural and

William Charlton

The Physical, the Natural and the Supernatural

Modern Ideas of Matter and Mind

Sheed & Ward
London

ISBN 0 7220 6810 7

First published in Great Britain in 1998 by
Sheed & Ward Limited
14 Coopers Row
London EC3N 2BH

Production editor Bill Ireson
Printed and bound in Great Britain by
Biddles Limited, Guildford and King's Lynn

Contents

Introduction

This book has two aims. The first is to describe the origins of our modern ideas of matter, mind, the physical and the supernatural. The second is to test the case for a view which many educated people today think irresistible: that only the physical (however that is to be defined) is truly real, that we can no longer find room for the supernatural, and that everything even in our own nature that is not open to scientific analysis is somehow illusory or subjective. This position is commonly known as 'physicalism'.

My two aims are connected. The belief that the physical exhausts the real goes with certain assumptions about the history of thought. The idea of the mind, it is supposed, has ancient and primitive roots. It arises from people's first consciousness of feelings of pleasure and pain, desire and fear. And people start by trying to explain everything that happens in nature by the causal intervention of gods and demons. But when they eventually pass from a religious to a scientific attitude towards the world, they find that human beings, like everything else, are structures of molecules, atoms and subatomic particles. They find these particles interacting with each other according to physical laws; nowhere do they see a mind or spirit interacting with anything. The conclusion seems plain. We may not yet know exactly how physical interactions in the brain give rise to subjectivity. Perhaps we shall never know this. But these interactions are the only true explanation of everything that exists and everything that happens.

This conclusion goes, as I say, with the assumption that our ideas of the psychological result from consciousness of feelings, together with the further assumption that the only genuine way of explaining reality is by means of causal interactions. I shall argue that both our notion of the mind and our notion of the physical are the work of the philosophers of classical Greece. Everywhere and at all times it has been assumed that people see and hear, that they have feelings and plans and that they are more or less intelligent. All adventures in human thinking set off from the certainty that we ourselves and the animals with which we are chiefly concerned act for reasons and purposes. But the modern notion of mind arose almost by accident. It was the unplanned child of Plato's efforts to persuade people to rely on reason and calculation rather than custom and guesswork, and to engage in intellectual pursuits instead of concentrating on sensual gratification. And the modern notion of the physical does not stare people in the face when they stop explaining the course of nature by supernatural agencies. The achievement of the Greeks was not to replace supernatural causes by natural ones; it was to look for any explanation of natural phenomena at all.

Science is so embedded in our society that we imagine everyone must want to explain what we find in nature, and everyone must have some idea of causal interaction. But nature does not ask us to explain its works. The natural supposition is that if something is natural it stands in no need of explanation. Neither does nature tell us what will constitute an explanation or offer us causal interactions as an explanatory ideal. The Greeks were the first people, so far as we know, to enquire why natural regularities exist, why kinds of action like heating and cooling have different natural effects on different things, and how we can give systematic explanations of things that are not due to human intervention. They devised and experimented with various kinds of explanation. Some of these can be grouped together as causal. And these, I shall try to show, fix the modern conception of the physical.

Somewhat as alcohol and raisins can be obtained from grapes, or butter and whey from milk, the notions of the physical and the psychological are abstracted by ingenious and sophisticated thinkers from a broad notion of the natural, a notion that spreads from the workings of the seasons at one end to conscious, purposive action at the other. Once this is realised, the physicalist picture seems far less compelling. Those who are most convinced that only the physical is real, will be found to have lost the primitive human grasp of the natural. To them, the only alternative to the physical is the supernatural, and they think that if psychology cannot be reduced to physics, it must be a seedy kind of theology. But if we see nothing between the physical and the supernatural our ideas of both will be distorted. We find our conception of the fundamental particles of physics becomes increasingly mathematical; they are emptied of causality, and causality migrates across to the supernatural, which then seems to consist of extraordinary but very powerful causal agents. As a boiler suit needs a human body inside it if we are to tell at a glance what is its top or bottom, its front or back – otherwise it is a crumpled heap – so the concepts of the physical and the supernatural need the concept of a purposive living organism to keep them in shape.

The plan of this book is as follows. Chapter One is a fanciful, mythlike picture of a population that has no systems of coercion and no literacy. Such populations actually exist in the world today – Joseph Pestieau's book *Guerre et paix sans état* has a map on its end papers showing where to find them.[1] But my chapter is not intended as a substitute for field anthropology. Its purpose is to show how people might engage quite peacefully and comfortably in social life with no concepts of existence, truth, being and not being, good and evil, pastness and futurity, or belief and desire. These notions which are now so much discussed by philosophers were all, I later claim, introduced by philosophers. We can get on quite well without them, and though they are here to stay, we must be careful not to assimilate them to the ideas we try to form about reality. Otherwise one of two things will happen. Either we shall think that they are correct ideas. In that case we shall soar off into a rhapsodic supernaturalism, and fancy that goodness and truth are things that exist, and thinking and existing are things that go on, in addition to the other things we have reason to believe in. Or else we shall think that they are incoherent, false ideas, that nothing is really good or bad and that thought is an illusion; in which case we relapse into a dreary physicalism.

That these philosophically interesting ideas are in fact the creations of philosophers, and in particular that the ideas of the mind and the physical were introduced by the philosophers of classical Greece, I argue in Chapter Three. These claims are contentious, and I have defended them at greater length and with more massing of scholarly material elsewhere.[2] But between the picture of the pre-philosophical innocents and the account of the work of the philosophers I have inserted a chapter on language. My reason is this. Language is the evidence of intelligence. Beliefs and desires are expressed in statements and orders, and an account of how words can acquire meaning and a relation to things beyond themselves ought to throw light on the nature of thought. Philosophers who hope to end with a physicalist account of human beings usually try to make out that people could acquire language through certain processes of conditioning. The drilling of army recruits provides a model, though not, as it happens, one philosophers often use. The recruits are trained to march, wheel, halt, etc., when they hear various shouts from the drill sergeant. They may also be habituated to do various things, fire a rifle, blow a whistle, drop to the ground, when certain circumstances arise. Physicalists suggest that it is by comparable processes of training that people grasp the meaning of an order or the meaning of a statement that something is the case. Language-learning then appears as a matter of becoming responsive to causal stimuli. Much has been said about this way of explaining how we come to understand the meaning of sentences, especially since the publication in the 1950s of the later work of Wittgenstein. I have offered some technical contributions to the debate in my book *The Analytic Ambition*[3] and elsewhere; here I discuss the issues in a dialogue. Plato asks about the origins of language in his dialogue the *Cratylus*. I call my Chapter Two 'The New *Cratylus*' partly in tribute to him (though his central question is about words, while mine is about sentences), and partly in memory of W. H. Mallock's *The New Republic*.[4]

In Chapters Four and Five I come to grips with some of the ideas that reinforce modern confidence in physicalism. One is the idea that a person's believing something or wanting something or feeling a sensation like pain should be conceived on the model of physical processes and states like burning or being liquid. If there really are mental processes and states, it is thought, they will have to be just like physical ones except that they are non-physical. Another is the idea (which also figures in physicalist theories of language) that thoughts can be modelled on naturalistic paintings; the content of a belief or desire is taken to be a kind of representation. Since these models are physical, the use of them leads inevitably to a physicalist theory of mind. And a third is the belief that not only is acting of our own free will compatible with physical determinism, but it actually requires that the movements of our limbs should be brought about, in accordance with information and instructions stored in the brain, by stimulation of our sensory system.

In Chapter Six I turn from the psychological to the supernatural. It is sometimes supposed that religion is a natural feature of primitive societies rather as crocodiles are a natural feature of some tropical rivers. The concept of it, we may think, is forced on ethnologists as the concept of perpetual cold is forced upon travellers in the Antarctic. I argue that in fact it is absorbed from Judaeo-Christianity and then projected onto other cultures. I also point out that biblical writers model the relationship of the natural to the supernatural on the relationship between the wild and the cultivated. Unlike the Greeks, these authors have little notion of causality. Their God is less a powerful causal agent than a skilful gardener raising natural life to a supernatural level. And his work belongs rather to the sphere in which people respond to invitations and act with regard for others than to the physical sphere of pushing, pulling and heating.

Chapter Seven argues that modern philosophers who want to abolish the supernatural are chiefly attacking impossibilities of their own creation: non-physical material and non-physical causation. But they also lack a theory of natural life that would enable them to make sense of Judaeo-Christian hopes for a supernatural life. And they conceive life after death in an individualistic way, whereas religious believers have often envisaged it rather as a sharing in God's existence.

In Chapter Eight I try to articulate the concept of God that appears in the Bible and in Christian prayers with the aid of psychological distinctions introduced by Plato. I show how the Platonic arguments for a tripartite human soul can be turned into arguments for a trinitarian deity.

Finally, I enquire into the kind of truth to which religious beliefs aspire. A significant number of philosophers and theologians today think that religious beliefs do not aim at literal or factual truth at all, but at the kind of truth sought by poets and novelists. If that is right, religious beliefs are perfectly compatible with physicalism. They are true in a sublime, poetic way, while in an earthy, literal way it is true that nothing is real but physical particles and their interactions. This happy reconciliation of physicalism and faith is not as new as is sometimes pretended. It is satirised brilliantly in *The New Republic*. In Chapter Nine I bring back the characters of 'The New Cratylus' to make my own contribution to the discussion. Professions of religious faith are certainly not like descriptions of distant stars or subatomic particles. But they are very like explanations of the reasons and purposes that other human beings have for doing what they do. Saying exactly what makes them true or false is not an easy task. But it is a task I approach from different angles in different parts of the book, and in this Chapter Nine I claim that a satisfactory account of truth about the existence, thoughts and intentions of natural persons like ourselves will also apply to truth about the existence, wisdom and will of God.

The book brings together work I have been doing since the publication of *Philosophy and Christian Belief* in 1988 and *The Analytic*

Ambition in 1991. Earlier versions of several chapters have appeared in philosophical journals as follows:

Chapter One: 'The Golden Age', *Epoche* 2 (1994).

Chapter Two: 'The New *Cratylus*', *Philosophical Writings* 4 (1997).

Chapter Four: 'Mental States and Physicalism', *Revue Roumaine de Philosophie* 38 (1994).

Chapter Eight: 'The Trinity and the Tripartite Soul', *New Blackfriars* 78 (1997).

I am grateful for editorial permission to reuse this material.

ONE

The Golden Age

It has been said that Spain and Africa were once all one landmass, and it is not so long ago, as geologists reckon time, since the Atlantic burst through the Pillars of Hercules. What an event must that have been! And for hundreds of years, what a spectacle, as the inexhaustible waters of the Atlantic poured into what was to become the Mediterranean over a waterfall incomparably higher and wider than any in the world today!

I do not know if that theory still holds the field. But let us suppose it true. And let us imagine that just a geologically few years ago what is now the southern Mediterranean was a warm and fruitful land, rich in sparkling lakes and rivers. It supported a population of primates that spent much of their time swimming and fishing. In the gentle climate they had little need of hair, and life was so undemanding that their time of playful immaturity became more and more extended. Like their simian ancestors and their cousins the lemurs and baboons, they exhibited a variety of forms of social organisation. Their communities ranged in size from nuclear families to groups containing a couple of dozen adults; and within the larger groups some lived alone, others in pairs, others in every possible permutation of male and female that allowed for sex and the rearing of young.

Hunting together, warning each other of lions, water-snakes and other menaces, gathering food for their friends and demonstrating

[8]

to each other their simple skills, they came to have increasingly complex expectations of one another. Signs to be stealthy, requests for social grooming and so forth were made in confidence that they would be so interpreted, and spontaneous sounds and gestures gave way to convention-governed speech. Accuracy in communicating with one another and ingenuity in using the resources nature provided seemed to help one another along. Both progressed briskly, and in a few generations they were building huts, making fish-hooks and drinking cups, and composing songs and stories.

The first human beings, as we must call them, had an excellent understanding of one another. No one was surprised to see a person going to a tree on which hung ripe mangoes, leaving a bathing pool at the approach of a crocodile, or sitting about on a clear, moonlit night in the company of a sexual partner. They were clever at solving technical problems in the manufacture of the objects they were accustomed to produce; and their practiced hands were guided by a good eye for form. They had nothing we should call a work of art; but they had nothing ugly either.

But while their intelligence was equal to ours, their knowledge was not. Natural selection had equipped them with eyes and ears that enabled them to find food, to evade predatory animals and to locate or avoid one another as need might be. But their senses gave them no information about anything smaller than midges (not that they had them in those fortunate latitudes) and only the most superficial facts about the contents of the sky. They distinguished many varieties of fruit, plant and animal, but their taxonomy was shifting and unsystematic. Autumn flowers were separated from spring flowers as much as from autumn fish. They had acquainted themselves with the uses and dangers of various substances that were to be met with in their vicinity. But the only kind of explanation they used was the kind that fitted their own behaviour and that of the more sagacious animals. Those natural processes that are not the product of intention most of them no more tried to explain in any way at all than they tried to fly. The few who craved useless knowledge speculated that inanimate objects like the sun, clouds, mountains and rivers have purposes, or that natural events are the work of unseen agents like the predators they blamed when their food, animals or children went missing in the night. That there might be some completely different way of explaining storms, the procession of the seasons or changes in the fish population, never occurred to anyone.

In the world as they saw it, the most conspicuous and substantial items were the members of their particular community and the individual persons and animals they cared about. Next in importance came predators and prey, and after that, useful and dangerous artifacts, organisms and substances. These tailed off into a material murkiness in which language ceased to bother about such ambiguities as 'Adam had a little apple'.

In the absence of written records, their knowledge of the past was restricted to what they could remember. The older people, of course, could remember more remote occurrences, and could also recall what they had been told by old people in their youth. But what no one could remember or could be remembered to have remembered was irretrievably lost, a subject at best for poetic invention; and there was a certain scepticism even about what people did claim to recall. That was partly because memory was recognised to be fallible, but it has also to be admitted that accuracy about the past was not an ideal.

Truth itself was not an ideal. They often wanted to know whether or not a friend had come or whether or not there were fish in a pool. They were concerned that their friends should be *au courant* with matters of practical importance. And they distinguished between ensuring this and deception. But they did not think that there is any general difference between what is and what is not the case; nor, therefore, between saying what is the case and saying what is not. They admired the reflections in water on windless days, but these failed to suggest a general model for truth. They might have been led to think of truth as some kind of exact correspondence with reality if they had cultivated naturalistic painting; but in those primitive times they had no painting at all, their decoration was abstract and stylised, and their mimetic impulses were channelled into dance and song.

Not only had they no general concept of truth; they had no general concepts of the past or the future either. At any moment they had some idea what had happened in the recent past and what would happen in the near future. They spoke of events as prior or posterior to the time of utterance, of an eclipse as having occurred the previous night, or a hunt as about to start next morning. But they had no grammar, they did not divide their speeches into distinct words, and the linguistic expedients by which events were related to the present went unnoticed. They had no words for the past or the future, any more than for the present or for existence. If their inflections of tense, their temporal particles and so on imparted a past or future tinge to things, as a stained glass window imparts colours to whatever is illuminated by it, they were unconscious of this. The past was a set of constraints, the future a set of agenda; neither was a field for knowledge.

Indeed, psychological concepts like knowledge, belief and desire were all alien to them. The explanations they offered had such forms as 'He has gone out for fruit for the children', 'She did not swim because of crocodiles', 'They fenced the yams against wild pigs', 'These flints are for arrows for small birds'. They relied on prepositions and inflections of case, occasionally on conjunctions and parataxis. But employing such devices unconsciously they were unable to speculate on what they expressed. Nobody said 'In "because of crocodiles" the word "because" expresses perceptual awareness or belief', or 'In "for fruit" the word "for" expresses purpose and introduces an object of desire'. Such utterances never crossed their lips, and general notions of volition, intention and cognition played no part in their thinking.

You might imagine that in a society which lacked these essential tools for the scientific study of the mind, mental illness and autism would be rife. But you would be wrong. Our forebears were as sane as we are, and no less perceptive about one another. Their minds were, so to speak, transparent to their relatives and friends. One person understood another's words and deeds directly in terms of the things the other believed to be present or absent, and of the outcomes the other wanted to promote or prevent.

The first human beings could hardly be expected to have had a legislature or a police force. These benign institutions are the marks of an advanced society. Their behaviour was regulated by custom. This usually started by governing the behaviour of parents and children, and went on to gather sexual partners and siblings into its net. In each of their small communities these relations were conceived as carrying positive and negative obligations, duties to do certain things and to refrain from doing others. For their productive work skills were passed down from one individual to another, but when the capital assets of the community were concerned, such as hunting grounds or cultivated land, custom was again in operation. As the social groupings were mutable, however, so were the customs. Individuals moved freely to groups with different customs or modified those they had received.

Even when they adhered most rigidly to custom and fulfilled their obligations meticulously this was not a blind, mechanical conservatism. The central relations of parenthood and sexual partnership were cemented with personal affection. They also had private friendships. As happened among their neighbours the vampire bats, these were strongest and most lasting among the females. In the larger groups the females found it easier to coexist with the males if there was a strong measure of inter-female solidarity. Where it was customary for males and females to act separately or work at different tasks, custom and personal liking often reinforced each other, and where custom chafed, two or three friends might leave a community together.

Both affection between individuals and habits of social co-operation contributed to the development of language and all that goes with language; but they worked in different ways. The discharge of customary duties gave our ancestors a sense of being integrated into a living organism. A person attending on a birth or death or watching over the domestic animals was aware of living with the community's life. Actions from which people had a duty to refrain filled them with a dizzy horror. On the other hand the object of benevolent concern was always an individual. I said that their minds were transparent to one another, but that did not make them aware only of the things their friends were thinking of, and not of their friends themselves. Rather, another intelligent or sentient being was something to be known primarily from the inside. They looked out through each other's eyes, felt through each other's hands, shared fears and pleasures. And it was in this identification with another person that they were most aware of their own existence, while the acts from which friendship required them to refrain were acts that threatened their grasp of who and what they were. Injuring or failing to help a friend seemed to divide them against themselves. They experienced pain and conflict, which often resolved into outright hatred of the former friend: a hatred that was not pleasant but not easy to terminate. Against such disasters otherwise pointless-seeming customs were cherished as fences.

But though they responded differently to the calls of friendship and to the duties of society, they did not think of either as such. Like mental states, moral obligations were transparent to them. If parental duty ordained that food should be gathered for your children as well as yourself, they thought that a sensible use of nature's prodigality. If it told you to keep an eye on your children when lions were about, that seemed a rational response to the presence of lions. Concern for your friend might whisper that you should gather food for her young as well as yours, or alert her to the influx of water-snakes: these would be further sagacious responses to the contingencies of your situation. What for us is acting as duty and friendship demand, to the first human beings was simply acting intelligently.

For this was the Golden Age, the age before things went wrong and bodyguards, law-enforcement and slavery were introduced; the age before literacy muddled people up and philosophy followed to freeze or resolve their confusions.

[13]

TWO

The New *Cratylus*

When Ursula Witherington invited her cousin Ligea Teikimokoino to stay with her, never for a moment did she expect the invitation to be accepted. So remote were the Iles des Nuages, where Ligea lived, that Britain was there supposed either to be a legendary place like Lilliput, or else to be part of the United States of America. Neither supposition was likely to result in anyone's knocking on her door. Miss Witherington felt rather a fool, then, when Ligea wrote to say she was coming for a week with her newly-wedded husband Ernest Vevekukumi.

Miss Witherington lived in a lonely house near the Scottish Border called Windyhaugh. The prospect of entertaining two young Polynesians for a week was more than she could contemplate on her own, and she sent an S.O.S. to her old friend Eddie Dodson. A tutorial fellow of an Oxford college, Mr Dodson was so set in traditional ways as to have his summer entirely at his own disposal, and immediately promised to come. His response brought relief but still not complete peace of mind. The Polynesians were unlikely to know what a tutorial fellow was, and might they not wish to see someone under sixty? By putting on three line whips she secured undertakings to come from her nephew Charles Hewlett and his girlfriend Sue.

She need not have been so apprehensive. Windyhaugh lay in a bend of the River Dyre where it meanders through a broad, open valley. The weather was excellent and the Vevekukumis were happy to spend all day swimming under water hunting fish. Ernest spoke hardly any English, but his manners were charming and he seemed to have a very serene temperament. Ligea's English was not too bad, and though her face was not conventionally beautiful she was extremely vivacious. They hit it off immediately with their cousin Charles, and Mr Dodson, who had lived among young people for forty years, soon got on terms of friendly banter with them.

'Take care what you say, Ligea,' said Ernest the second evening at dinner, after Ligea had addressed some rather impertinent remark to Mr Dodson. 'He is a university professor!' [The conversation must be imagined as taking place mainly in French.]

Ligea: A university Professor! I am terrified! From now on I shall be completely silent.

Mr Dodson: I'm not a Professor. I'm just an ordinary Fellow of my college.

Miss Witherington: In England it isn't chic to be a Professor.

Ligea: But you teach?

Mr Dodson: Yes.

Ligea: What do you teach?

Mr Dodson: Philosophy.

Ligea: My God! What is that?

Charles: That's right. Now you've got him. I have noticed that there's nothing philosophers dislike so much as being asked what philosophy is.

Ligea: But why?

Charles: Because they don't know the answer.

Ligea [laughing]: Is that true, M. Eddie? That you teach philosophy and you do not know what it is?

Sue [in English]: I had a friend who did philosophy. He said it was all about the meaning of words – la signification des mots [for the benefit of the Vevekukumis].

Ligea: But that is the affair of philologists. Is there no difference between philosophy and philology?

[15]

Mr Dodson: I think Sue's friend had in mind linguistic philosophers. They believe that how we talk about certain things is the
best guide to how we think about them.

Ernest [chuckling]: They must be simple fellows, those philosophers. Do they believe everything they hear?

Ligea: How ignorant you are, Ernest! Philosophers believe nothing.
They are very scientific, very sceptical. [To the table] Ernest
never went to school if he could help it. He preferred to go fishing.

Mr Dodson: I'm afraid you flatter us. But it is only certain words
and ways of speaking that philosophers consider.

Ligea: What words? Would a philosopher know the meaning of any
Eoenanian words? [Eoenanian was the ancient language of the
Iles des Nuages.]

Mr Dodson: It would be an advantage to him if he did. Ursie has
told me something about it, and it seems a fascinating language.
The words philosophers are most interested in are words that
don't appear both in European languages and in Polynesian.

Charles: What words are those?

Mr Dodson: 'To be,' and 'To have,' for example. You don't have
such words in Eoenanian, do you?

Ligea: No.

Charles: Then how do you say 'We do not have that in our language?

Miss Witherington: Let me see if I can manage that. `A`o`e tena `i
to matou `eo. [General applause.]

Charles: What a lovely language. You must teach it to me, Ernest.
Are there any words that you have and European languages
haven't?

Miss Witherington: There's '*pekiau*'.

Charles: What does that mean?

Miss Witherington: A *pekiau* is a second husband, usually younger
than the principal husband. Isn't that right, Ernest?

Ernest: You should ask an anthropologist. They occupy themselves with that sort of thing.

[16]

Ligea: And philosophers too. That is what M. Eddie says.

Mr Dodson: Not exactly. There isn't a European word for a second husband because we don't have second husbands in Europe, not official ones, at least. The Eoenanian words that philosophers are interested in aren't words for things they have in Polynesia and not here. They're words like '`a' and '`e' which aren't really words for anything.

Charles: '*A*' and '*e*'?

Miss Witherington: '`*A*' and '`*e*', with an 'accent', what in English we call a 'glottal stop'.

Sue: A glottal stop? What's that?

Miss Witherington: You hear it in London sometimes. [Attempting Cockney] "I, Charles, pass that bo'le along. When it reaches you it seems to ge' roo'ed.'

Charles [exaggerating the glottal stops]: '`A' and '`e', then. But if they aren't words for anything, how can you be interested in their meaning? Isn't the meaning of a word what it stands for or denotes?

Sue: No, that's wrong. I said that to Julian – he's the friend I mentioned just now – that what a word means is what it stands for; and he said there are lots of words, I think he gave 'not' as an example, which don't stand for anything, but they still mean something because they affect what a sentence means. So knowing the meaning of a word is knowing what difference it makes to the meaning of a sentence.

Mr Dodson: Magnificent. He was well taught, that Julian. I don't suppose he was one of my pupils?

Sue: No, he was at Warwick.

Charles: Never mind about Julian. What difference do '`*a*' and '`*e*' make?

Mr Dodson: I believe '`*e*' does the work of future inflections of tense, and . . .

Charles [seeing Sue's eyes glazing]: Be gentle with us, Mr Dodson.

Mr Dodson: Please call me Eddie.

Charles: Thank you. But you must remember that Sue and I belong to the post-grammatical generation. The facts of language were hidden from us at school for fear they'd spoil the purity of our style. If anyone had used words like 'inflections of tense' in class he'd have been told to go and wash his mouth out.

Ernest: Why?

Ligea: Have you not noticed? The English take great care of their teeth – look at Sue and Charles. When we have children we must tell them to wash their mouths out.

Mr Dodson: What I should have said is that '`e`' makes a sentence refer to the future, and '`a`' makes a sentence a command. Is that right, Ligea?

Ligea: Yes. You understand Eoenanian perfectly.

Mr Dodson: And that shows the difference between being past or future and being pink or blue. There are words for colours, but there are no words for past or future, for having been or being on the point of being. '*A été*' and '*sera*' are not such words. If they were, you would have them in Eoenanian.

Ligea: I can see, at least, why we have no philosophy in Eoenanian.

Charles: Wait a bit. We're supposed to know the meaning of a word only when we know the meaning of a sentence. But how do we know the meaning of a sentence like 'I shall go fishing tomorrow'?

Mr Dodson: Perhaps Sue can tell us.

Sue: It's obvious, isn't it? We know the meaning of 'I' and 'fishing' and 'tomorrow', or we look them up in a dictionary, and work it out from that.

Charles: Yes, but your friend Julian says you discover what a word means by seeing what difference it makes to put it into a sentence. That means you must already know the meaning of the sentence before you can work out the meaning of the word.

Sue: Oh, shit – [blushing] *merde*, I mean. I always hated philosophy.

Charles: Philosophy's all right. It's just that particular *moche* theory of Julian's.

Mr Dodson: Is it really so *moche*? Couldn't we start by grasping the meaning of some simple sentences as wholes?

[18]

Charles: How do you mean?

Mr Dodson: Well, you've seen those hospital films where there's a dying patient on the operating table, and the surgeon, nurses, anaesthetists and so on are all standing round, looking tense. 'Scalpel,' says the surgeon, or 'forceps,' and a nurse hands him a scalpel or forceps. 'More oxygen,' he says, and the anaesthetist twiddles the taps on the oxygen cylinder. The team in the operating theatre have learnt what to do when the surgeon makes certain sounds: isn't that the same as grasping the meaning of orders?

Charles: The nurses only understand 'scalpel' as an order to pass a scalpel because they understand sentences like 'That's a scalpel.'

Mr Dodson: Well, let us imagine a group of people fishing in some beautiful place like the Iles des Nuages, and one of them says 'Shark' – what's the Eoenanian for a shark?

Ernest: There are many different kinds of shark around the Iles des Nuages. A small shark is a *moko*; a great white shark is a *mako*.

Mr Dodson: Good. Suppose someone once says '*Mako*' when there is a great white shark in the vicinity, and the practice grows up that when there's a shark there you make that sound, and when there isn't, you don't. Young fisherman learn that practice when they learn to fish. Then '*Mako*' is like a sentence, and when a young fisherman grasps the practice, that is like grasping the meaning of 'There's a great white shark there.' Perhaps that is how language started in the Iles des Nuages.

Charles: What do you think of that theory, Ligea?

Ligea: I do not like it.

Mr Dodson: Why not?

Ligea: Your fishermen and nurses, they are learning how to please people and avoid being blamed. But what has that to do with language?

Mr Dodson: How do you mean?

Ligea: Your nurse knows that when the surgeon says 'Scalpel' she must pass a scalpel or everyone will curse her. But why should she think that making the sound 'scalpel' is saying anything? She knows that if she has a patient whose temperature rises suddenly, she should call the doctor; but she does not think that becoming feverish is saying something. When I learnt to sail I learnt that if the wind rises I must take in sail and if it changes direction I must move the tiller. Otherwise the boat might capsize. Is the wind speaking to me?

Mr Dodson: No. But the wind does not rise or change direction on purpose.

Ligea: If I am fishing I know that I must not shoot off my spear unless there is a fish there. Otherwise Ernest will reproach me. I fire my spear on purpose. But that is not the same as saying 'There is a fish there.'

Mr Dodson: What is the difference?

Ligea: When I say 'There is a fish there,' I can say 'There is no fish there.'

Mr Dodson: Isn't that like not firing a spear?

Ligea: Saying 'There is no fish there,' is different from saying 'There is no boat there,' or 'There are no children.' Is doing nothing to be equivalent to all these things?

Miss Witherington: There is no wine at this end of the table.

Mr Dodson: You see? There is a sign it is safe to make only in the situation in which there is no wine at your end of the table.

Charles: You call that a situation? It seems to me more of a non-situation, the bottle's not being where my aunt wants it.

Mr Dodson: But perhaps Sue's theory doesn't really require us to grasp the meaning of sentences as wholes. I can know what difference a word makes to sentences without knowing the meaning of any particular sentence in which it is used. Ligea confirms that '`e' makes the same difference to an Eoenanian sentence that 'will' makes to the English sentence 'Tomorrow it will be fine.' Knowing that, I know what '`e' means. But I don't know the meaning of a single Eoenanian sentence. The theory isn't that we first grasp the meaning of a sentence and then work out the meanings of the parts, though I think that is also a defensible thesis. The essential idea is that we must first grasp the concept of the meaning of a sentence [*la signification d'une phrase*] before we can grasp the concept of the meaning of a word.

Charles: The concept of the meaning of a sentence? I'm not sure I grasp that at all. I suppose sentences occur in novels and poems. Are you saying that to grasp the meaning of a sentence is to know what difference it makes to a poem in which it appears?

Mr Dodson: No, the theory is rather that sentences are the primary bearers of meaning. We can attribute meaning to words on the one side and poems on the other only because we can attribute it to sentences.

Charles: But do sentences have meanings in the same way as words?

Mr Dodson: Why shouldn't they?

Charles: Well, even if words like 'not' and 'future' don't stand for anything, you admit that words like 'red' and 'white' do. 'White' signifies something and 'wine' signifies something. But I don't see that there's anything the sentence 'This wine is white,' signifies. [Miss Witherington was a hostess who believed in serving different wines with different courses. They were now at the pudding, for which she had provided Muscatel, and the table was dotted with decanters and bottles of red and white wine like a chess board in the end game.]

Mr Dodson: Are you sure? Consider the words 'the double of'. If we add a further word like 'two' or 'three' we get a complex expression for a number. 'The double of two' signifies the number 4; 'the double of three' signifies 6.

Ligea: Now you are talking mathematics.

Mr Dodson: Not for long. You can treat the words 'is white' like the expression 'the double of'. If you put at the beginning 'This wine' or 'this salt' you get a complete sentence which expresses something true or false. So why not say that as 'the double of three' signifies a number, so 'This wine is white' signifies something true or false?

Ligea [who has unfinished claret]: Certainly 'This wine is red,' signifies something true in the way 'Twice three is six' signifies something true. 'Is red' is like 'is equal to two times three'. I agree with Charles. 'Red' and 'white' and 'twice three' are expressions for things, but 'Six is twice three' is not, and neither is 'This is white'.

Charles: Of course, 'That wine is red,' is not devoid of sense. But I do not think we need the concept of sentence-meaning to be able to ask about word-meaning. Many of us post-grammaticals have never heard of sentences. But put a menu in front of us in a French restaurant and we ask 'What does *"grenouille"* mean?' And to understand the answer, all we need is the humble concept of a frog; we don't need the de luxe concept of the meaning of a sentence.

Mr Dodson: Citizens of your post-grammatical world can ask what a word means without knowing what a sentence is because when they learn to speak they are shown printed words with spaces between them. But before the Europeans came to the Iles des Nuages, did your people have the concept of a word?

Ernest: We had names, that was all.

Mr Dodson: And even if someone does have the concept of a word, it is one thing to know what a frog is, and another to know that *'grenouille'* is a word for a frog. To know that it is a word for a frog is to know that when you say to the waiter *'Grenouilles!'* frogs are what you are telling him to bring; or when you are walking in the country and say *'Grenouilles!'* frogs are what you declare to be present. Unless you have the notion of a statement or an order you will not be able to think that the word *'grenouille'* signifies anything.

Charles: So by *'la signification d'une phrase'* you mean a statement or order?

Ligea: But that is obvious. What it signifies is what it wants to say [*veut dire*] and I know that when I know what it affirms or commands.

Mr Dodson: Is that right, Sue?

Sue: What? Sorry, I was thinking of something else.

[22]

Charles: That everything comes back to ordering and asserting and things like that. There are these basic linguistic acts, and if you want to explain how anything has meaning, from single words to complete epic poems, you must do it in terms of them.

Sue: I suppose so.

Mr Dodson: Is that what Julian said?

Sue: No, actually he said something different.

Mr Dodson: What did he say?

Sue: He said that truth was the fundamental concept.

Mr Dodson: More fundamental than asserting or ordering?

Sue: I think he said it was basic.

Mr Dodson: Good. Then let's base something on it.

Miss Witherington: Don't go on at her, Eddie. She's not your pupil. I expect the idea was that the purpose of speech is to tell the truth, or something like that.

Sue: No, it wasn't that. Julian said – I'll have to say it in English – we know what a word means when we know what it does to a sentence, and we know what a sentence means when we know what would make it true.

Miss Witherington: That's marvellous, Sue. What a memory you have for this stuff. No wonder Eddie would like to be your tutor.

Mr Dodson: I don't think there's a don in the world that wouldn't like to have Sue for a pupil.

Sue: Thank you.

Charles: So the new theory is that understanding a sentence is knowing, not in what circumstances you can utter it without being reproached, but in what circumstances it is true. Do you like that better, Ligea?

Ligea: No.

Mr Dodson: Why not?

Ligea: I sometimes say 'Where is my handbag?' or 'Leave the keys in the car!'

Ernest: She talks like that all the time.

Ligea: Ernest understands my sentences, but he does not know what would make them true. Nothing would make them true.

Mr Dodson: But he does know what would make true the corresponding statements, 'The keys are in the car,' 'Your handbag is in the pirogue.'

Ligea: I would never take my handbag in a pirogue.

Charles: You want to explain understanding a question or a command in terms of understanding a statement. Why not the other way round? I understand what someone says when he says 'You are drinking Muscatel,' because I understand what he orders when he says 'Drink Muscatel!'

Mr Dodson: Perhaps affirming things or declaring is the basic kind of speech, and we have to do something additional, use a special tone of voice, say, to ask a question or give an order. But Sue's new theory doesn't really require us to say that statements are primary. It's enough if statements, questions and orders all have something in common. 'Are you drinking Muscatel?', 'You are drinking Muscatel,' and 'Drink Muscatel!' all express something that is true if you are drinking Muscatel. But the first asks if it is true, the second says it is true, and the third tells you to make it true.

Ligea: What is this thing? Muscatel?

Mr Dodson: That you are drinking Muscatel.

Ligea: Perhaps drinking is a thing, a function. But that I am drinking Muscatel, that is not a thing. Besides, it is only the affirmation 'You are drinking Muscatel,' that says that I am drinking Muscatel.

Mr Dodson: But that, at least, is saying something true or false?

Ligea [who is still drinking claret]: Something false, yes.

Mr Dodson: So there is some false thing which it presents as true, and you know the meaning of the sentence when you know what that false thing is.

Ligea: I do not understand. I know what Muscatel is, and what drinking is, but I do not know what this false thing is, unless it is just your affirmation.

Ernest: That is because you are not a philosopher. It is as if M. Eddie were telling you about Canada, about Baffin Island. 'What are these polar bears?' you would say, 'These glaciers and ice-floes? I have never seen them.' No, we do not have them in the Iles des Nuages, but explorers have seen them. M. Eddie is an explorer in the soul, in language. He has seen these false things, many of them.

Mr Dodson: You can think of a sentence as a kind of representation in words. I could produce a picture of a house and say 'That's what my house is like,' or 'Build me a house like that!' Saying something true or false is like producing the picture, and affirming is like saying 'That's how things are.'

Ernest: In England you have very beautiful pictures of houses. We had no pictures at all in the Iles des Nuages before the Europeans came.

Mr Dodson: Didn't you have tattooing?

Ernest: That was not like European pictures.

Miss Witherington: It was more like heraldry.

Ligea: Perhaps we did not know what pictures are before the Europeans came, but we do now. You say, M. Eddie, that these true or false things are like pictures?

Mr Dodson: That was the suggestion.

Ligea: Pictures of what is true or false?

Mr Dodson: Perhaps. Or of what is or is not the case.

Ligea: But you cannot have a picture of what is true in that way, a picture of something true. A picture of a house, yes, of something beautiful, yes, of Ernest drinking Muscatel, yes; but a picture of that Ernest is drinking Muscatel [*une peinture de qu' Ernest boit*], no.

Miss Witherington: But we do say that a person can give a true or false picture.

Ligea: A true or false picture *of something*. But a true picture of Windyhaugh would be a false picture of our house in Tuaivinui. You cannot have a picture that is true or false *tout court*. But M. Eddie is not talking of what is true of Ernest and false of me. He says that a sentence, even a sentence like '*Ligea, bois ton muscat,*' or '*Est-ce que Ligea boit du muscat?*' expresses a truth or falsehood.

[25]

Mr Dodson: Yes, the same thing as '*Ligea boit du muscat*'; or do you not think that even that sentence expresses something false?

Ligea: If, as you said M. Eddie, we understood the sentence as a whole, perhaps it would, but Charles and I did not agree to that, and I do not agree about what is common to '*Ligea, bois ton muscat*' and '*Ligea boit du muscat.*' What is common is that in both you speak of drinking Muscatel. But in the first you speak of it in telling me to do it, in the second by affirming that I am doing it. We understand the sentences if we know what is spoken of, and in what manner, in what kind of speech.

Mr Dodson: Well?

Ligea: Drinking Muscatel would be bad for me, because it would make me dizzy. So if you tell me to drink Muscatel you advise badly. But what you advise is not bad absolutely – it is not bad for Ernest – but bad for me. And if you affirm that I am doing what I am not doing you speak falsely, *tu mens*, but you do not affirm something false absolutely, you affirm of me what is false of me.

Mr Dodson: So you want to say that absolute goodness and truth attach to what Charles calls 'linguistic acts' like declaring and commanding . . .

Charles: Or to believing and wanting. What Ligea says will apply to them too.

Mr Dodson: . . . but not to things that are declared or commanded or believed or desired: what enters into the content of a speech or thought can be good only for something or true only of something.

Ligea: Yes. And even when I affirm something, it is not the same to know what thing I am affirming and what conditions must be fulfilled if I am to speak truly. Suppose I say '*Mea meitai te meika.*' You understand my sentence if you know that I affirm that bananas are good. But do I speak truly? That depends. Perhaps it is true to say that bananas are good if I am planning a meal, or if I am a European painter looking for a subject for a picture. But it is false if I am telling Ernest how not to become fat.

[26]

Mr Dodson: Perhaps, though I think you have chosen too easy an example if you are right that absolute goodness attaches only to orders and desires. You could probably have managed with whatever is the Eoenanian for 'Bananas are yellow.' But you and Charles, I think, want to make acts like affirming and ordering fundamental. To understand what a word like 'drink' or 'sweet' signifies is to know what we affirm or order when we use it in the appropriate construction. So what is affirming? What is ordering?

Ligea: I do not know. You tell me. You are a philosopher.

Mr Dodson: But most philosophers agree with Julian that the fundamental notion is truth.

Ligea: What difference does that make? Can we not ask them what it is to assert?

Mr Dodson: What a pity Julian isn't here. I'm sure he could help us. Did he ever say anything to you about assertion, Sue?

Charles: Julian is a broken reed . . .

Ernest: *Un roseau cassé?* What does that mean?

Ligea: It is a very *grossier* remark. Charles has no shame.

Charles [blushing]: I meant let's leave Julian out of it. Eddie's just mentioned a lot of other philosophers. Perhaps if we asked what they have to say we should get on.

Miss Witherington: Perhaps we should get on to the drawing room if you've finished discussing your wine.

Charles: We'll take it with us – the wine and the discussion.

Mr Dodson [to Ligea as they go through]: They are making *calembours*. That is a favourite form of English wit.

Ligea: *Calembours?*

Mr Dodson: A kind of *jeu des mots*. They are rare in French because the language is so precise, but I'm sure you have them in Eoenanian.

Ligea: Ah yes. And in the Iles des Nuages I think philosophy would be thought a *jeu des mots*.

Mr Dodson: It is here. But in England we take our games more seriously than anything else.

[27]

Ligea [in English, flirtatiously]: Now you are making game of me. [Laughing at his surprise] But before you go any further, you are going to tell us what the philosophers who agree with Julian say about asserting and ordering?

Mr Dodson: Very well. When Ursie said to us just now 'Go to the drawing room,' what did she hope to achieve by that performance?

Miss Witherington: I hoped to get you to move to the drawing room.

Mr Dodson: I suggest that, more precisely, you hoped to excite in us a willingness to move to the drawing room.

Miss Witherington: Perhaps. What about statements, then?

Mr Dodson: Suppose I say 'It will be sunny tomorrow': what purpose could I have in saying that?

Ligea: To give an example, evidently. To answer Cousin Ursie's question.

Mr Dodson: Yes, but we're interested in the weather, aren't we?

Ernest: Certainly. If it is fine tomorrow, we go fishing; otherwise we go to Edinburgh to buy presents.

Ligea: So you say 'It will be fine tomorrow,' to make us want to go fishing? No, that is too complicated.

Ernest: If M. Eddie says it will be fine, I think he wants us to believe it will be fine.

Charles: You mean that saying it will be sunny is doing something in order that we may believe it will be sunny? What happens if we put a lot of wooden ducks on a pond in order that real ducks may think it's a safe place to swim about?

Ernest: Do you do that in England? It is a fine idea.

Charles: Yes, but we don't imagine we are affirming to the ducks that it is a safe place to swim.

Mr Dodson: No, because we don't expect the ducks to understand why we're putting out the decoys. But I not only utter the words 'Tomorrow it will be fine,' in order to implant or activate in Ernest the belief that it will be fine; I rely for success in this project on his divining that that is my purpose. In this case surely I *affirm* that it will be fine.

Charles: All right. And taking that refinement as understood, the theory is that affirming and ordering are acting in order that the bystanders may believe things and desire things?

Mr Dodson: Rather a convincing theory, don't you think?

Charles: That remains to be seen. What are believing and desiring?

Mr Dodson: The philosophers I have in mind would call them 'propositional attitudes'.

Ligea: Propositional attitudes?

Mr Dodson: Attitudes we adopt towards propositions.

Ligea: But what are propositions?

Charles: It is a *grossier* expression. Philosophers make propositions to their pupils when they have no shame.

Ernest [to Ligea, in a low voice]: *E aha?*

Ligea [likewise, to Ernest]: *Hakafaufau.*

Mr Dodson [uneasily]: Now Charles *se joue de nous.* Propositions are the true or false things we affirm and believe.

Charles: I see; they are your polar bears and ice-floes. I suspected as much. So our task, Ligea, is to give an account of affirming and ordering which dispenses with them.

Ligea: You mean that we agree that speaking is trying to influence thought [*pensée*], and I know what you mean [*veux dire*] when I know how you want to influence my thought, but instead of these pictures of what is true or false we talk of things we all know, like wine and fish and flavours?

Charles: Yes, and Windyhaugh and the Iles des Nuages.

Ligea: But that is easy. In the Iles des Nuages we drink the same wine all through the meal. But Cousin Ursie gives us different wine with different food. And what decides whether or not we drink a wine is its flavour. Chablis is good with trout because it is dry; Muscatel is good with *gateau* because it is sweet. Ernest is eating *gateau*, he is thirsty, he sees a bottle, he starts to reach for it. Then fear seizes him. The wine is white, perhaps it is Chablis and will taste bitter. '*Courage*' says Cousin Ursie, '*doux*'. She wants the sweet taste of Muscatel to come into his mind as a reason for taking the wine; and she knows he will guess she has used the word '*doux*' for this purpose.

Mr Dodson: But what if he is eating trout? Then she says '*Attention! Doux!*' to stop him taking the wine.

Ligea: But the sweet flavour is still to be his reason. Both times she says it is true of the wine that it is sweet, and saying that something is true of a wine, or true of you or me, is acting in order that that thing may enter your thought as a reason.

Mr Dodson: You said earlier that we can say that wine is sweet only if we can say it is not sweet. How is the flavour to enter your thought then?

Charles: Wouldn't Chablis' not being sweet be a reason for drinking it with trout? '*Courage*' we say, '*pas doux*'.

Mr Dodson: Is that right, Ligea? That we sometimes act in order that not being sweet or not doing something should enter someone's thought?

Ligea: No. There is no such flavour as not sweet. But something can be a reason by its absence. Off our islands the sharks are not dangerous, but in the Tuamotos they attack people. It is only if they are absent that Ernest and I would dive there for langoustes. If they were present we should not leave the boat. So Ernest would look carefully over the side. And he might say '*Pas des requins*' in order that I may know that because they are absent it is safe to dive.

Charles: Whereas if he says '*Pas des langoustes*' you will know it is useless to dive. I think I shall stick to the Iles des Nuages.

Mr Dodson: So in the Iles des Nuages speech begins not when people learn to adopt attitudes to polar bears, but when they act in order that flavours and sharks and so forth should come into people's thought in certain ways. These ways being?

Charles: A flavour or a marine creature can be a reason either for doing something or for not doing it, and it can be that either by its presence or by its absence.

Ligea: We see people act for these reasons. But sometimes they do not act, and then we make signs to them.

Charles: And naturally they come to understand why we are making these signs, and we come to depend on their understanding.

Miss Witherington: Charles, would you mind passing round the drinks?

Mr Dodson [while Charles does this]: How do people come to understand that sort of utterance in the Iles des Nuages?

Charles: I suppose they see people looking thirsty. What will you have, Aunt Ursie?

Miss Witherington: Whisky for me, please.

Ligea: May I have orange juice?

Charles: Certainly. What about you. Sue?

Ernest: I think that Sue is asleep.

Charles: How extraordinary! What on earth can have sent her to sleep? I'll wake her up.

Miss Witherington: No, don't.

Charles: I'll give her a shake.

Miss Witherington: Don't shake her, don't shout at her, don't do anything.

Mr Dodson: Perhaps Ligea would say that you are to make it false of her that she awakens.

Ligea: Certainly if we let M. Eddie draw us into more philosophy, we shall make sure that she continues to sleep.

Charles: But it is not more philosophy. It is just finishing the philosophy we already have.

Ligea: Well then, M. Eddie, when Cousin Ursie forbids Charles to wake Sue, yes, I agree that she wants the condition of being awake to come into Charles's thought. But not as something true or false of Sue. As something bad for her.

Mr Dodson: Bad [*mauvais*]?

Ligea: In Eoenanian we say '*mea pe*'. Disagreeable, at least. And when she told him to pass the drinks there was a situation of glasses near to hands that she wanted to seem good, *mea meitai*, to him.

Mr Dodson: You mean she wanted him to desire it?

Ligea: If he thinks it good he will desire to bring it about, he will want to move the glasses near to our hands. But we can act to bring something about only if we can also act or do nothing *for fear that* it should come about. What can figure in our thought as good can also figure as an object of fear or aversion.

Charles: And in the Iles des Nuages, once they see that things can function as positive and negative goals, they act to make them do this.

Ligea: Because we are practical. And if we act in order that what is good may be a goal, or in order that what is bad may be feared, we order and counsel rightly.

Mr Dodson: Whereas you speak truly . . . ?

Ligea: If we act in order that what is present may be a reason by its presence or what is absent by its absence.

Mr Dodson: But in Eoenanian you have no word for being present or being had?

Ligea: No.

Mr Dodson: So how then do you explain the difference between speaking truly and speaking falsely?

Ligea: In the Iles des Nuages we all know the difference. It is only European philosophers that must have it explained to them.

THREE

The Origins of the Mind-Body Problem

In a passage from which many later discussions have started, Descartes says:

> I have on the one hand a clear and distinct idea of myself insofar as I am only a conscious, not an extended thing, and on the other hand a distinct idea of a body insofar as it is only an extended, not a conscious thing; so it is certain that I am distinct from my body. (*Meditations* 6)

Descartes was certain, in fact, that the entire contents of the universe can be sorted into two categories: there are bodies, and there are minds; and minds have attributes and activities of one sort, psychological ones, while bodies have properties and movements of a completely different sort, physical ones. This opinion was widely held in the seventeenth century. So level-headed an Englishman as Locke believed that there are two kinds of substance, material and spiritual. And even today people beginning to study philosophy are swiftly convinced of an urgent need to enquire whether there really are minds and mental states as well as bodies and physical events, and, if so, how the two are related. This is called 'the mind-body problem'.

Although there now seems, at least, to be this chasm in the world, plunging down as far as we can see, the earliest writings that are preserved for us, whether from Greece, Palestine or the East, show no awareness of it. These writings contain many words for such things as walking, running, swimming, sleeping, dying, fighting, speaking, weeping, laughing, drinking, fishing and other things people do; but these things are all, in modern terms, psychosomatic. There are no words for anything purely mental. When Achilles in Homer deliberates whether to cut down Agamemnon, his liver is agitated in two separate directions in his hairy front (*Iliad* 1. 188–9; see also *Odyssey* 6. 139–47). Aeschylus, trying at the beginning of the fifth century to describe the inscrutability of the divine mind, speaks of 'very overgrown, shadowy passages in the midriff', *dauloi papridon daskioi te poroi* (*Supplices* 93–103). And societies without any physical science can hardly be expected to have a vocabulary for the aseptically physical.

How, then, did reality get split? It is sometimes imagined that Descartes did it in the work from which I have just quoted. I shall argue that the notions of mind and body emerged in Ancient Greece, chiefly in the century from 450 to 350 BC. And I shall start with the concept of the body, because that is apt to seem quite straightforward and unproblematic.

In fact it depends on the concepts of matter and the physical. That statement sounds surprising because the concepts of matter and the physical are advanced and sophisticated, whereas the most primitive people have concepts of head, hands, legs, etc., which we count as parts of the body. But let me say what I mean by 'the concept of the body'.

We use the English word 'body' in a number of ways. We use it for corpses. 'Burke and Hare,' we say, 'had bodies. And working, as they did, by flickering lantern-light, they must sometimes have swapped bodies without noticing it, Burke taking Hare's body and Hare Burke's.' This notion of a corpse really is primitive and no anthropologist has yet reported a tribe too backward to possess it.

'Body' is also used for a person's trunk or torso. 'Medusa's face,' we say, 'was rather a turn-off, but she had a beautiful body', or 'I'm sorry, madam, we stock lipstick and nail-varnish but not body-paint.' This anatomical or cosmetic notion of a body is simple and primitive too.

When we pass from the dissecting room or the beauty parlour to the physics classroom, we encounter quite a different use of the word. 'Bodies in motion keep moving,' says Mr Newton, 'bodies at rest stay put.' 'Are electrons bodies?' asks a clever pupil. 'Well,' (a bit shiftily) 'they're more like bodies than shadows or fields.' By a 'body' a physicist means something composed of material of some kind which behaves in accordance with certain laws. Clearly, this notion is not primitive; it presupposes the existence of some kind of physical science.

When I talk of the 'concept of the body' I have in mind the notion we use in saying things like, 'We all know that we have bodies; it's only religious people who are sure they have souls,' and 'I wonder if it would really be possible for you to take my body and me to take yours. Perhaps I simply *am* my body.' Clearly, this is neither the resurrectionist's nor the beautician's notion. Is it the physicist's? I am so fortunate as to have quite a number of bodies in the physicist's sense – a handkerchief, a toothbrush and so forth; but when, in a philosophical discussion, I say 'my body' I am not referring to any body like this I can put in a jumble sale. It is a philosophical problem precisely what I am referring to. The answer I find most plausible is that I am referring to myself *viewed from the physicist's point of view*: my body is the particular human being that I am, considered precisely as a material or physical body. If that is correct, then this notion of the body, though it is not the physicist's, depends upon it, and cannot exist in a society that has no notion of physical science.

If we wish to find its source, then, we must enquire into the notions of matter and the physical. These arose when the Greeks initiated the project of explaining natural phenomena.

It is often supposed that the most primitive savages try to explain natural phenomena; the Greeks were not the first people to make an attempt, but the first people to make a good attempt, and look for scientific explanations instead of just religious ones. Before examining this opinion, I had better say what I mean by a 'natural phenomenon'. I mean anything that is not due to human intervention, intelligence or folly. So wars, universities, knitting and economic crises are not natural; but stars, clouds and living organisms are natural; so are eclipses, rainbows, wind, ice, blood and digestion. When I strike a match or stick a knife into an enemy, my movements are not so much natural as more or less skilful. But that the match bursts into flame, that blood gushes from my enemy, are natural consequences of these intentional movements.

Such being natural phenomena, is it true that every society tries to explain them? For practical purposes to say that something is natural is to say it does not need explaining. What puzzles us is what seems to be an exception to the natural order; and once we see that it is natural after all, we usually cease to be puzzled. If in a primitive society you persist in asking, 'But why do stones released from on high fall to the ground? Why is fire hot? Why does the sun rise and set?' you risk being told 'Don't be a fool. They just do.'

Alas, it may be said, that is not how it is in reality. Look at the first chapter of Genesis in the King James version:

> God said, 'Let there be lights in the firmament of the heaven to divide the day from the night, and let them be for signs, and for seasons and for days and years . . . ' And it was so. And God made two great lights, the greater light to rule the day, and the lesser light to rule the night; he made the stars also. (Gen 1.14–16)

The sun, moon and stars are natural phenomena: surely this is an explanation of them. But not a scientific one. We are told that God made them in order to divide day from night and serve as a sort of calendar for human beings. The Old Testament Jews were no more ignorant and superstitious than the inhabitants of the African rain forests or the mountains of Irian Jaya. So, without more ado we can generalise and say that all human beings uninfluenced by the

Greeks try to explain all natural phenomena in supernaturalist, teleological terms.

The chapter from Genesis mentioned above is untypical in telling us for what purpose God made the stars; the Old Testament usually speaks of God's purposes as unfathomable. Apart from that, the chapter chiefly wants to insist that the whole natural order is the product of God's intention. The whole natural order, however, is not itself a natural phenomenon. To us, the coming into existence of the sun and moon were natural events, like the coming into existence of a lake after heavy rain. I doubt if early readers of Genesis were sure that the sun and moon came into existence at all; they may have thought both that the natural order depends on God's intention and that it has always existed. They certainly will not have thought of the coming into being of a heavenly body like the sun as a natural event calling for explanation. The Old Testament does not reveal a lively curiosity about specific natural events ('Why does water freeze in winter?' 'Why does smoke rise up and rain fall down?') together with a supine willingness to be content with the same explanation ('Because that is God's will') for all. Rather, it reveals a lack of curiosity about specific phenomena combined with a firm belief that God is the author of the whole business.

It may be added that the first chapter of Genesis, the Psalms, the Book of Job and other biblical writings that attribute nature to God are not now considered the products of simple nomads. It is extremely rash to assume that other civilisations, much less that primitive societies generally, should have the same views as they express. The question whether the whole natural order depends on anything is a sophisticated one which need not occur even among people curious about specific phenomena. It seems to have occurred to Plato; but the ancient Greeks generally did not attribute the whole natural order to anything, and neither, so far as I am aware, did the civilisations of the East.

The so-called Presocratic Philosophers from the sixth century onwards do try to explain natural phenomena. But their explanations are of various kinds, and ideas of what constitutes a satisfactory explanation develop.

We are told that Thales said that all things arise out of water, and Anaximines that cloud arises out of air, water out of cloud, and earth out of water.

These theories give us the ancient concept of matter. Everyone has concepts of various sorts of material, water, air, gold, milk, etc., but the general concept of matter is different: that arises only when a philosopher notices .that the concepts of water, air, gold, etc., have something in common. What they have in common is the explanatory role they play, but they play more explanatory roles than one, and different philosophers fasten on different ones. Aristotle noticed that they are said to stand to other substances and to objects like coins and lakes as 'that out of which'; and he used the word *hule* – which we translate 'matter' but which was simply the Greek word for wood that had not yet been cut up or worked upon – to label them: they are *hule*- or matter-concepts.

That the general concept of matter does not force itself on us naturally can be seen from the fact that Aristotle's concept was not quite the same as ours. For him, the matter of something is that out of which it arises, and it is obvious that everything does arise out of something. Our notion, in contrast, rests on something that is not obvious. We believe that just as a wall consists of bricks and an old-fashioned kitchen chair consists of pieces of wood, so a brick or a piece of wood consists of molecules, molecules consist of atoms and atoms consist of subatomic particles like electrons and protons. For us, the matter of something is something present in it like the parts in an engine. Whereas for the Greeks primitive matter would be stuff out of which other things arise, which does not itself arise out of anything further but has always been there, for us it is constituents of which other things are composed that are not themselves composed of further constituents. To people without microscopes, water, blood, gold and even bronze would appear to be primitive kinds of matter by our criteria; they do not seem to be composed of anything further, unless we say that a cubic foot of bronze is composed of 1,728 cubic inches of the same stuff. But they are not primitive by Aristotle's criteria, in that they arise out of other things.

Perhaps it will be thought that saying, 'Natural things arise out of water,' though it tells us something about them, is hardly explaining them. I do not think we should ban the use of 'explain' here. Even when it is used unexceptionably, it is applied to widely different things. Explaining a property of right-angled triangles is not the same as explaining a human action and explaining eclipses is different from both. But certainly telling us what a thing arises out of is not telling us very much. Even if water does arise out of air or blood out of food and drink, we may want to know why they arise out of these things – that is, what is responsible for the occurrence and brings it about. Presocratic thinkers offered answers to such questions of various kinds.

It is part of acquiring a skill to understand that certain action by a human agent has a certain result – blowing on a fire, for instance, makes it burn brighter. Some thinkers applied this kind of explanation to natural phenomena: they appealed to unskilled, mindless causal agents and causal action, postulating agents and action that could not be perceived on the model of those that could. We are told that Anaximines in the sixth century said, 'Rainbows arise because rays of the sun, falling on thick, compact air, cannot pass through.' (Anaximines, Fragment A 18.) We see the rays of the sun and the thick clouds; we do not see exactly how they interact, but he attributes rainbows to their interaction. Empedocles, writing in the mid-fifth century, has charmed modern readers by the model he uses to explain breathing: a little girl playing with a sort of hollow pipe she dips into water. When she closes the top with her fair hand and dips the pipe into the water, no water enters; as she removes her hand, the water flows in. If she covers the top again, she can take out the pipe with the water in it, but if she again removes her hand, the water gushes out and air rushes in. (Empedocles, Fragment B 100.) The pipe, the water and their interaction are all visible. Empedocles postulates unseen pipes in the body that fill with blood and empty, and suggests that the movements of the blood in these pipes cause air to be breathed in and out.

In an atomic theory, atoms are unseen causal agents the interactions of which are offered to explain perceived phenomena. Although the Greeks did not in general accept an atomic theory as we do, one was proposed in the fifth century by Leucippus and Democritus. Unfortunately, no fragments of their exposition of it survive, but there is a fairly well worked out atomic theory in Plato's *Timaeus*. The ultimate constituents here are right-angled triangles, but these occur in nature only joined together to form regular solids. They form four solid figures, cubes, tetrahedra, octahedra and icosahedra. Plato makes these figures particles, respectively, of earth, fire, air and water, and explains by means of them a wide range of natural phenomena. Substances formed of large, uniform icosahedra are not liquid but fusible, and when fire-particles penetrate them, they are separated and divided into smaller particles, and this appears as melting. Smaller icosahedra which, when mingled with fire-particles form a liquid, when separated from fire and air condense into ice, snow and frost. Water-particles mixed with earth-particles constitute clay, and when they are driven out by fire, the remaining earth-particles condense into pottery.

> Someone who, for the sake of recreation, puts aside discussion of eternal things and considers probabilities about things that come to be, will obtain a pleasure that brings no regrets and endows his life with a moderate and judicious kind of play. (*Timaeus* 59 c–d)

Not liking the tone of this and similar remarks, some scholars make Plato out to have been an enemy of empirical science. But his atomic theory has very much the character of the physical theories of that golden age of modern science, the seventeenth century. The triangles of which Plato's particles are formed are triangles of nothing at all except extension. The particles move about, but apart from that they are just geometrical solids. His aim is to show that natural phenomena can be explained without attributing to particles any properties not definable in mathematical terms. Like Descartes, Plato dispenses with gravity as a fundamental force. Fire cuts because fire-particles, being pyramid-shaped, have sharp acute angles; it is hot because it cuts into our bodies; it is lighter than water because its particles are smaller. Why a small particle of extension or space should be lighter than a large one, why something shaped like an adze or an axe should divide things more easily than something shaped like a golf ball, geometry cannot tell us and Plato does not ask himself. But since the seventeenth century, philosophers and philosophers of science have cherished the belief that the ultimate explanation of everything that happens lies in the microstructure of reality, and of this belief Plato is the earliest and most eloquent exponent.

While the Greek atomists wanted to explain natural phenomena by unseen agents endowed only with mathematical properties, medical practitioners appealed to active and passive causal powers. Plato was aware of this explanatory strategy too, though he himself prefers to apply it only to non-physical phenomena like rhetoric, and gives us a good description:

> See what Hippocrates and the truth say about nature. This is how we should think about any nature. First, is that about which we wish to become skilled and otherwise capable single or multiform? Then, if it is simple, look at its power. What is it by nature such as to do to what, or to undergo under the action of what? Or, if it has several forms, enumerate them, and see this about each taken separately, what is it such as to affect and how is it such as to be affected by what? *(Phaedrus* 270 c–d)

It is one thing to explain chemical processes in terms of mathematical structure, hoping that causal powers will eventually be seen to arise out of microstructure, and another to explain health and disease by the causal powers of food, parts of the body and so forth without appealing to structure. But these two kinds of explanation are similar in character. It is not easy to say exactly where the

[41]

resemblance lies, but that we feel it is shown by our calling them both 'causal'. They give us the rudiments of the concept of the physical. For we consider them both physical modes of explaining, and we consider a phenomenon physical insofar as it can be explained in either way.

In Aristotle we find these kinds of explanation connected with the notion of matter. That out of which something arises, according to him, besides accounting for the thing itself as its matter, as 'that out of which', also accounts for some of its behaviour. It can do this in at least three ways. It accounts for how the thing affects other things on which it acts: this cocktail makes you drunk because it arises partly out of gin. It accounts for how the thing is affected by the action upon it of other things. When you apply a red-hot poker to a candle, the candle melts because it arises out of wax. And it accounts for certain movements the thing makes independently of its being acted upon by anything. A pot which is released from on high falls to the ground, or to prevent it from falling to the ground we have to exert upward pressure on it, because it arises out of earth. Any explanation which appeals in any of these ways to the notion of the material of a thing is also, by our reckoning, causal and physical, and we might say that an object or substance is physical just insofar as its behaviour can be explained in terms of its material.

We human beings, then, are physical objects insofar as our behaviour is explainable causally in any of these ways, by the geometrical properties of our components, by causal powers, or by the substances out of which we arise; and the notion of the human body which is contrasted with the notion of the mind depends on a grasp of one or more of these kinds of explanation.

So much for bodies. We do not find them already there as we find mosquitoes already there when we go to the Greenland icecap; our idea of them is a consequence of our having worked out and found useful certain ways of explaining natural phenomena. What of the mind? That too is a human invention, though it was invented in a slightly different way.

[42]

Today, we draw a broad distinction between mind and matter, or between the psychological and the physical, and a further, narrower distinction within the field of the psychological between the mind and the senses, between intelligence and sentience. The broad distinction seems to us more important, and we may imagine that it would naturally come first. But it does not. Clearly, until people have a clear conception of the physical, they cannot form an idea of that in us which goes beyond the physical; neither can they group together as being non-physical certain human functions and states.

New Testament writers sometimes oppose spirit (*pneuma*) to body or flesh, but on examination this turns out to be not the broad contrast but the narrow. For Paul, the body is not just matter moving mechanically; it has desires of its own. 'Let not sin reign in your mortal body, obeying its desires' (Rom 6.12); 'I see another law in my limbs, campaigning against the law in my mind' (Ibid., 7.23); 'If you live according to the flesh, you will die, but if by the spirit you impose death on the actions of the flesh, you will live' (Ibid., 8.13). And sometimes, instead of the word 'carnal', 'of flesh' (*sarkinos*) he uses 'psychical', 'of soul' (*psuchikos*): 'What is sown is a psychical body, what is raised is a spiritual body' (1 Cor 15.44; cf. 2.41 and 3.1). Psyche is what distinguishes the animate from the inanimate; it is what we share with animals. So what seems at first to be the contrast between the psychological and the physical proves to be the contrast between rationality and animal passion.

Paul writes in his epistles as Plato writes in the *Phaedo*. Plato starts by saying that death is the separation of soul and body (*Phaedo* 64 c). But it soon appears that by 'the body' he does not mean what philosophers mean today (Ibid., 64–6). The body 'gives us endless trouble with its search for necessary food'; it 'fills us with desires, fears and all kinds of illusions' – that is, it causes in us the visceral feelings of hunger, lust and bodily fear, and its sense-organs are constantly misinforming us. Neither does the soul merely direct the body as a driver directs a motor car. It 'opposes its feelings, . . . correcting some of them with punishments, some

[43]

with exercises or medicines or, less violently, with threats and counsels, and holding debate with its desires, rages and terrors' (Ibid., 94 b–d).

Plato starts by distinguishing rational from non-rational motivations, but he does not end there. He notes that the fallacious deliverances of the senses can be corrected by calculation and measuring, and he proceeds to separate out intellectual operations which are not influenced by the state of our sense-organs from sensory functions that are determined by them. His purposes were moral or practical. He wanted people to set time aside for the more purely intellectual functions, and to order their lives generally in accordance with reason and calculation, not in obedience to local prejudice or instinctive desires and aversions. But his distinction had two unforeseen consequences of considerable importance. It created the subject matter of philosophy and the general concept of thought. The story of how this came about is complicated but illustrates graphically how the consciousness of language influences cultural history.

The human functions which Plato fancied and which we call 'intellectual' were expressed loosely by the verbs 'calculate', 'compare', 'go back over' (*logizesthai* or *analogizesthai, sumballein, epanienai*). But more accurate descriptions require verbal phrases consisting of a verb of saying or thinking and some further expression. Comparing is thinking larger, smaller or equal, thinking similar or dissimilar, sometimes thinking better or worse. Rational evaluation, as distinct from merely finding pleasant or unpleasant, includes thinking useful or harmful, expedient or inexpedient, beautiful or ugly, just or unjust. Counting and measuring, processes on which Plato relies to supply what is lacking in sense-perception, involve applying concepts of number, thinking things one or many, and if many, then some definite number or multiple. Identifying and differentiating are thinking the same and other. And intellectual thought is pervaded by judgements of what is real or unreal, what is the case and what is not the case.

Primitive people, of course, have all these thoughts. But they have them more or less unconsciously, in the course of hunting, gathering, courting, making war. And it is part of being primitive to be illiterate. If people do not have writing they will not have grammar, or divide sentences into words. If they do not think of sentences as constructed out of words, they cannot differentiate verbs like 'say', 'declare', 'think', 'judge' from words that are used with them like 'equal', 'like', 'other', 'many', 'good''; still less can they pick out linguistic items like 'is', 'not', 'was', 'becomes', 'for' or inflections of number, case, tense, mood, etc. And if they do not differentiate these items, they cannot think that there are things signified or expressed by them. They may think there are such acts as evaluating and comparing; but they can hardly think there is such an act as thinking, much less that there are such things as good, equal or being.

Plato was associated in his youth with two pioneers of linguistics, Cratylus and Prodicus. He had a clear insight into how sentences are constructed, and was conscious of all the elusive linguistic items I have just mentioned. As part of his crusade to promote rationality, he repeatedly calls attention to the things expressed by words that combine with verbs of thinking: words like 'similar', 'one' and 'good', and verbs of being and becoming. These, he says, are things over and above, or 'separate from', the things expressed by words like 'horse', 'ox', 'clay' and 'finger'. His utterances to this effect have often been interpreted as expositions of an amazing theory. This theory (known as 'The Theory of Forms' or 'Ideas') is supposed to be that outside space and time, in a superworld of their own, there really exist such entities as the Form of Being itself, the Form of Largeness, and the Idea of Good. It is one of the ironies of history that a campaign – and in fact a brilliantly sucessful campaign – for making people value reason and guide their lives by it, has been construed as a rhapsodic flight into what is wildly unreasonable and practically unintelligible.

A first unintended consequence of Plato's efforts was the emergence of the discipline we call 'philosophy'. The Greeks used the word *philosophia* for any kind of enquiry or research that went

[45]

beyond what was customary and practically necessary. Until the fifth century, most Greeks set rather a low value on *philosophia* in this sense. Not so Plato, and he championed it so effectively that it has been part of our civilisation ever since.

But what Plato and his contemporaries called *philosophia* we now, in tribute to him, call 'academic study'. What we call 'philosophy' is one academic discipline among others, the study precisely of the peculiar things, embedded in our thought and speech, to which Plato called attention: the comparative notions of equality, similarity, etc., the evaluative notions of the just, the beautiful, the useful, etc., the arithmetical notions of unity and number, the ontological notions of being, not being, becoming, having been, etc., and certain others to which I shall come in a moment. It is fair to say that primitive people have no conception of these things whatever, and nothing can be discovered about them by research in the way things can be discovered about human history or about physical nature. But they are the main business of those persons employed by universities in departments of philosophy. Am I implying that but for Plato, universities would have no such employees? It would be truer to say that if Plato had not identified these topics and found them fascinating, there would be no universities at all.

A second unforeseen consequence was the recognition that there is such a thing as thinking. Having separated off the words that combine with verbs of thinking and enquired into the things they express, we are left with the verbs of thinking themselves. Do they express something too? G. E. Moore says somewhere that thought is 'diaphanous', and the metaphor is apt. If I see a friend, I see through my seeing directly to the friend; if I feel a longing for a glass of wine, I am not disinterestedly conscious of my desire, but just avidly conscious of wine. We are aware of *objects* of perception, wanting, repugnance and so on, and our awareness of these things is like a perfectly clear sheet of glass through which we see, or like the optic lens, something we never see and most people do not even know they have. We become aware of a glass window if we breathe on it, or if the glass is not clear but coloured. The things studied by philosophers – goodness, excess, otherness, etc., – are not hot air breathed on thought by Plato and his followers so much as stains intrinsic to the windows of the human soul. Plato found himself confronting a generic concept of thought which would cover all the modes of intellectual activity he wanted to promote; and hence he found himself having to deal, not only with the concepts I mentioned earlier, but with a further range of concepts, those of thinking, perceiving, imagining, wanting, etc.

Plato tackles psychological phenomena in a variety of ways, of which two especially have contributed to the concept of the mind. In a series of brilliant images and analogies in the *Republic* he models intellectual thinking on seeing. As sight stands to natural organisms and substances illuminated by the sun, so intellectual thought stands to the things signified by his favourite linguistic items, rendered intelligible by something rather mysterious which his later followers identified with God but which he himself characterised in terms of goodness and unity. And besides modelling intellectual thinking on seeing, he models objects of thought generally on naturalistic paintings, suggesting that thought or consciousness is a matter of having non-physical pictures presented to the mind.

It is here that we see the birth of the modern concept of the mind. To have that concept is above all to have a general notion of consciousness or awareness, a notion which is not restricted to intellectual thought but extends to sentience. Because of the diaphanous nature of consciousness, nobody (it seems to me) had this general notion before Plato. The ideas that thinking generally is like seeing, and that the objects of thought are like pictures except that they are non-physical, are integral to our concept and are plainly introduced by Plato. Plato was not acutely conscious of a problem about how the physical and the psychological are related – his discussion of perception in the *Timaeus* shows a regrettable blindness to the difficulties – but the terms of today's problem are present in his work, and not present in anything that precedes it.

I said earlier that Plato 'recognised' that there is such a thing as thinking; and I accepted a sheet of glass, clear or stained, as a

[47]

model for it. But that model is a physical one, which is bound to set anyone enquiring into the nature of thought on a path to a physicalist account. If we do not want to arrive at a reduction of the mental to the physical, and we cannot think of any non-physical model, perhaps we should question whether there really is such a thing as thinking after all, at least in the way I suggested. The reasons for saying that thinking exists are no better than those for saying that being exists. In both cases we have (at least in European languages) a verb. The verbs are related, for if I think the Parthenon beautiful, or think it smaller that St Peter's, I think that it *is* beautiful and that it *is* smaller. Thinking is thinking that something is the case, or thinking it is not, or wondering if it is, or wishing that it were. Insofar as there are different kinds of thinking, they are bound up with different kinds of being – evaluating is a different kind of thought from differentiating only if being good is different from being other. But in a way, there is no such thing as being. Certainly it is a bad mistake to suppose that there is such an activity or state as being there or existing – one in which Socrates indulged and from which Sherlock Holmes refrained. When that ontological pit seems to yawn at our feet, it is good tactics to say: there is no such thing as existing, but only such a way of thinking as thinking of something as an actually existing individual. When it seems to us that there is such a thing as being conscious, and we wonder how we do it, a psychological pit opens at our feet. What should we do then?

The first thing is to jump back, and say that it does not follow, because there are such things as comparing, evaluating, reasoning and generalising, that there is such a thing as just being aware. Having recovered our balance we can then look for a completely different strategy for getting insight into the obvious fact that we are aware of things. And we do not need to look outside classical Greece.

I have said how Aristotle thinks that matter can be a source of change. He contrasts the matter of an object with its form, and holds that its form can be a source of change in as many ways as its matter. One of these ways provides us, I think, with the strategy we want; but before explaining it I must explain what Aristotle means by the words *eidos* and *morphe* which we translate 'form'.

If the matter of an object is primarily that out of which it arises or of which it consists, its form is what arises out of this or what consists of this. We conceive a house as a shelter for human beings and their possessions, constructed out of bricks, beams, tiles and so forth, and consisting of these in a certain arrangement. Bricks, beams and tiles are the matter, in Aristotle's terminology, of the house; it is awkward to say that a shelter, or anything else, *is* the form – scholars who say of anything that it *is* a form find themselves sinking into a technical morass called 'the problem of universals', – but the word 'shelter' describes the form. Similarly, human beings are sentient, intelligent, purposive agents consisting of flesh, bones, nerves, etc. Although we do not arise out of flesh in the way pots are made out of clay, flesh and bone account for our falling when defenestrated and burning when flung into a furnace as the material of a pot accounts for its falling when released and breaking when struck. 'Flesh, bone and nerves', then, is a description of the matter of a human being, and 'sentient, intelligent purposive agent' describes the form. The word 'form' can be misleading here, because if I describe the shape my daughter must give herself in order to appear on the catwalks, in Aristotelian terminology I am not describing the form of a model girl but the matter. For an Aristotelian philosopher, a model girl is a means of displaying new fashions in dress (form), consisting in a young woman with certain proportions (matter).

As matter can account for change in three ways, so, Aristotle thinks, can form. The difference is that change has its source in form only insofar as it occurs for a purpose, only insofar as we can explain it, as we say, not causally but teleologically. The bricks of a house are placed in the arrangement they are by the skill of the builder who knows that the corners, window-spaces, etc., must be built in a certain way if the house is to stand up and function satisfactorily. Skill or craftsmanship is a source of change, not in the

[49]

craftsman but in something else like bricks or clay, rather as heat, in Aristotle's chemistry, is a source of change in the things on which it acts; but with the difference that a change is due to skill only insofar as it occurs because it is necessary for a purpose – the purpose, that is, of the craftsman.

Next, Aristotle believes that organs develop in plants and animals, and the organisms grow to their normal size, because this is necessary if they are to survive and reproduce. Insofar as these processes take place for this reason or purpose, they are due to the organism's form or nature as a living thing of a certain species. An organism's form is a source of its development much as its matter is a source of its moving downwards when released from on high, except that for a process in an organism to be due to its form it must occur not only *with* benign results, but *for the sake of* them. What we classify as biological processes, no less than the processes of skilful manufacture, are explained by Aristotle in terms not of causes but of goods to be achieved and evils to be avoided.

Finally, when we move or stay still on purpose, the changes which take place in our limbs, Aristotle feels able to assume, occur because they are necessary for our purposes, and to that extent they are due to our form or nature as sentient, intelligent beings. The difference between these processes and the biological ones is that these occur because of contingent circumstances which make them necessary or advantageous, whereas biological processes occur independently of circumstances; all human embryos develop hands, all elephant embryos trunks. Not that biological processes are not affected by circumstances at all; but they are affected by them as the downward movement of a stone is affected by impressed forces; the circumstances may modify or disrupt them, but do not elicit them. When, in contrast, we act because of what we perceive or think is the case, our nature is responsible for our responding to the objects of our awareness rather as a thing's matter, in Aristotle's system, is responsible for how heating, buffeting, etc., by other things affects it.

It will be seen that what we might call the 'psychological' is here given a place in a larger system embracing on the one hand biology and on the other the arts and crafts. And perception, belief and consciousness appear not as phenomena to be explained, nor, strictly speaking, as explanatory factors, but rather as links between such factors and what they explain. Just as causation is not itself a natural phenomenon to be accounted for but what connects natural phenomena with the things that explain them in one kind of explanation, so consciousness is not a natural phenomenon but something that connects certain phenomena with the things that explain them in another kind of explanation. As causation is what connects changes in things with explanatory factors we call 'causes', so consciousness or awareness is what connects purposive action and inaction with reasons.

Aristotle may be asked: 'Can one and the same movement be explained in both of these two ways? Is it possible both that I move in order that I may avoid some harm and also that my movement is caused by action upon me by some causal agent? Or if the first explanation is correct, has the movement no cause? Must it, at least, be other than the inevitable effect of some action upon the agent?' So long as these questions are outstanding, there remains a problem about the relationship between the physical and the psychological. But that problem is now located as one about the relationship between two ways of explaining a single phenomenon; it is not a problem about the relationship between two heterogeneous classes of phenomena. For thought no longer makes a separate appearance. There is no such thing as awareness over and above acting intelligently or foolishly.

Whatever merits the Aristotelian strategy may seem to have in the present physicalist age, it was not pursued after his death. From the fragments of his immediate successor, Theophrastus, we can see that people had great difficulty then, as they have now, in accepting Aristotle's view of biological processes. It is not obvious that his ideas on explanation have to be accepted as a package; but we do not find later thinkers trying to combine an Aristotelian treatment of sentience and intelligence with a non-Aristotelian biology; rather Hellenistic psychology teeters between Platonism and the physicalism of the Stoics.

Hellenistic and mediaeval readers of Aristotle might have paid more attention to the discussions which crop up here and there in his works of the interrelations of causal and teleological explanation, if they had been seriously bothered by the mind-body problem. In fact that problem seems to become acute only in the seventeenth century. Then it appears that matter is waiting in nature to be revealed by the microscope, while the notion of mind is the subjective effect of physical interactions between sentient beings and their environment, forced upon the most primitive people every time they experience a bodily sensation, though requiring the acumen of philosophers to determine whether it is a notion of anything that really exists in addition to these physical interactions themselves. When the terms of the mind-body problem present themselves like that, we are predisposed to a physicalist solution. Less so, if we see that the notions of mind and body are both inventions of a civilised society, classical Greece, which nevertheless remained dormant for nearly two thousand years before erupting into trouble like cancerous tumours under the incautious prodding of Descartes and his contemporaries.

FOUR

Mental States and Physicalism

In one of Preston Sturge's charming films the heroine says of the hero, against whom she is temporarily incensed, 'I need him like the axe needs the turkey.' I do not know if that is a common American figure of speech; but it aptly expresses the physicalist's need for mental states. Physicalists who say that the mind is nothing but the brain, need mental states to identify with brain states. Physicalists who say the mind does not exist at all, and describe themselves as 'eliminativists', need mental states to eliminate. Deprived of mental states to axe, the physicalist is likely to be left speechless.

What do I mean by 'physicalism'? Since its motives are often political – the physicalist thinks that evil laws or practices are getting support from supernaturalist beliefs – it can appear in various forms. Today it is usually presented as a thesis about explanation. One way to formulate it would be to say that everything that happens in the world, and in particular all the utterances and bodily movements of sentient and intelligent beings, have their source in matter and only in matter; but not many physicalists use this Aristotelian notion of matter as a source of change. A simpler formulation would be that causal explanation is the only genuine kind of explanation for actual occurrences. Not for everything.

Nobody looks for a causal explanation of the fact that if a number is divisible by three, the digits which express it add up a number divisible by three. The facts of arithmetic and geometry are to be explained not causally by logically. But all our actions, our utterances and, if they exist at all, our thoughts have causes that account for them as physical phenomena generally are accounted for by causes; and if teleological explanations are to claim validity, they must be reducible to causal explanations or at least imply that what they explain is also causally explainable. This statement of the physicalist thesis too might fail to satisfy some physicalists, because the notion of causal explanation on which it depends is problematic. But there are certain paradigms of explanation (I use 'paradigm' in its ordinary sense, not in any technical sense peculiar to philosophers of science) which are generally accepted: scientific explanations of things like eclipses and rainbows. Physicalists claim that there are things that explain every thought, word and deed as reflection of sunlight from drops of water explains rainbows and the movements of the earth, moon and sun explain eclipses.

Since few people immerse themselves in general reflections about explanation, physicalism is not a popular view; but it finds favour with many philosophers. In what follows I shall try to say why. It might be thought that that is an easy task. Just as the success of Euclid in explaining so many geometrical facts led Descartes to believe that everything can be explained logically, as a matter of logical necessity, so the success of seventeenth-century scientists in explaining various physical phenomena is surely what has led people to think that everything (except the facts of mathematics) can be explained physically, as a matter of physical necessity. But I do not think people are really as simple-minded as that would suggest. They have reasons, apart from the success of scientists in explaining some physical phenomena, for believing that this kind of explanation must apply to everything; and more important, people must already have a certain notion of the mental before the project of applying physical explanation to it can occur

[54]

to them. I shall argue that the concepts of a mental state and a mental process inevitably force physicalism upon people. I shall also suggest that some of the considerations responsible for these concepts of the mental have also contributed to the conviction that only physical explanations genuinely explain. We fancy that the kind of explanation that satisfies our curiosity about rainbows and eclipses is waiting in nature to be discovered for consciousness, that like oxygen or germs it is there for scientists to find. But that is an illusion.

Up to a point, my position is anticipated by Wittgenstein:

> How does the philosophical problem about mental states and about behaviourism [he could have said 'physicalism'] arise? The first step is one that altogether escapes notice. We talk of processes and states and leave their nature undecided . . . The decisive movement in the conjuring trick has been made, and it was the very one we thought quite innocent.[1]

Wittgenstein does not tell us why talking of processes and states in this way is the decisive movement in the conjuring trick, but it is easy to see what might prompt such a claim. Our paradigms for states and processes are physical: being spherical, being three feet apart, moving, rising in temperature. If we believe that thinking is a process or a state, consciously or unconsciously we are using physical models for the psychological. That alone will produce a tension in our conception of the mind which can be resolved only by some kind of physicalism. What is more, using any kind of model for a thing inevitably directs us to seek the same kind of explanation for the thing that we seek for the model; so if we model thought on physical states and processes we find ourselves automatically looking for the kinds of explanation and understanding of it that we have of physical phenomena. If physicalism is what I have just said, we are already unconscious physicalists.

Whether Wittgenstein would agree that this is what he meant, I do not know. He has a way of making one feel that whatever interpretation one were to offer of his words he would scornfully reject it. At any rate he does not provide the accounts I shall now provide of why philosophers believe there are mental states and processes, and why this is a mistake. There are two sorts of thing philosophers suppose to be mental states: bodily sensations like pain and what are sometimes called 'propositional attitudes' such as beliefs and desires. Non-philosophers tend to keep the expression 'mental state' for more dramatic phenomena: panic, despair, jealous rage, being utterly astounded; but philosophers might say that these mental states are somehow made up out of sensations, beliefs and desires. I shall argue that bodily sensations are states but not mental, and beliefs and desires are mental but not states.

That bodily sensations are mental is an extraordinary view which perhaps no non-philosopher has ever held. But Wittgenstein gives 'a pain's growing more or less' as a paradigm of a mental process.[2] And pain is taken as an uncontroversial example of a mental state by many distinguished philosophers who have written after him: Donald Davidson,[3] Richard Rorty,[4] Saul Kripke,[5] Paul Churchland,[6] and Peter Carruthers.[7]

If pain is a mental state, and if other mental states can be modelled on pain, it is easy to argue that mental states are identical with physical. The following argument is taken from *Holistic Explanation* by C. A. Peacocke.[8] Every physical event has a complete explanation in a series of prior physical events, and nothing has more than one complete explanation. But some bodily movements are explained at least partly by sensations of pain: if I touch something painfully hot I recoil. So these sensations must be identical with parts of a series of physical events. Obviously this argument shows that some mental states are identical with physical states only if sensations of pain are mental states.

Whereas Peacocke uses the assumption that pain is a mental state to show that mental states are identical with physical, Kripke uses the same assumption to show the opposite. His argument[9] runs like this. It is essential to a state of pain to be an object of aversion for its own sake, independently of what causes it or what it indicates: pains are necessarily hateful. It is not essential to any physical state to be an object of aversion. So a pain cannot be identical with a physical state.

Pain is certainly a paradigm of a bodily sensation. Other bodily sensations are sensations of warmth and coolness, sensations of hunger and thirst, sensations of sexual excitation. These are generally agreed to differ from such mental states as knowledge, belief and desire in that they give us no knowledge of things, are non-representational, have no 'intentional content'. I shall confine myself to pain, but what I say can easily be extended to these other sensations. Pain is certainly caused by such modes of physical action as cutting, burning, pressing with a thumbscrew, stretching on a rack. These causes result in bodily conditions that are naturally called 'painful'. Why should we think that pain, or a painful sensation, is anything else but such a bodily state?

Perhaps it will be replied that these bodily states are not themselves sensations of pain, but cause such sensations: they are called 'painful' because they cause pain, just as raw carrots and jogging are called 'healthy' because they cause health. Of course, the bodily states cause other things which are not mental, such as screams and movements of recoil, but the sensation of pain is a causal link between the burning or racking and these physical reactions.

If a sensation is not the bodily state but an effect of it, should we conceive it as a non-bodily state of which we are (at least usually) aware, or rather as our awareness of the bodily state? It would be natural to say that these bodily states are self-intimating: like pneumatic drills they make us aware of them; and because we are aware of them, we cry out and try to be rid of them. So shall we say that the sensation is the awareness of the bodily state?

If so, it will certainly be mental. But such awareness as we have of our bodily state when we feel pain is awareness of it as something to be shunned or changed for its own sake. I see no grounds for distinguishing this kind of awareness of the bodily state from aversion to it and desire to change or shun it. If someone under an anaesthetic is aware of a bodily state of being cut or cauterised

[57]

without being aware of it as an object of aversion, I would deny that there is a sensation of pain. Hence, if painful and pleasant sensations generally are identified with modes of awareness of bodily states, they will turn out to be a subclass of aversions and desires. That, however, is not how we conceive them. Desires and aversions are desires for and aversions to definite things; unlike bodily sensations they have intentional content. And painful and pleasant sensations are surely things we want to get rid of or retain; they are objects of aversion and desire, not themselves aversions or desires.

Are they, then, non-bodily states of which we are aware? If pain is an object of awareness at all, awareness of it must, I think, take the form of aversion to it for its own sake and desire to be rid of it. If a masochist desires sensations of pain, that will surely be just because they are also, and primarily, objects of aversion. But now, if pain is a state awareness of which takes the form of aversion, why should we think that this is anything other than the bodily state caused by the burning or racking which we try to change by medical treatment? Some justification is needed for introducing a further state that is causally dependent on this, especially as nobody has ever been able to conceive of a mechanism by which a physical state can cause a state that is non-physical.

But what kind of necessity is it, that awareness of a painful sensation should take the form of aversion? Is it a natural necessity, a necessity lying, *à la mode de Kripke*, in the nature of the thing? I suggest it is merely logical, like the necessity that a reward should be given because it is a benefit that has been deserved or earned. If I cure a hunter-gatherer's child of fever, and he gives me a beautiful gold nugget he has picked out of a stream, it is not essential to the gold nugget that it should be given to me; but we use the word 'reward' in such a way that if it is true to say 'It is a reward' it must be a thing given for a certain kind of reason. I claim that by 'pain' we mean a bodily state of an organism of which the organism is aware as an object of aversion for its own sake. That organisms are aware of some of their bodily states as objects of aversion and others as objects of desire is just what we mean when we say they are sentient: that is what sentient life is.

Some philosophers may think that we know by introspection when we are in pain that we are aware of something non-physical which is essentially evil. Certainly when I am conscious of being in acute pain, something is very clear to me; but how can I be sure that what is clear is the intrinsic evil of the thing I am aware of, rather than just the strength of my aversion to it, the vehemence of my desire to be rid of it?

So much for pains and their non-cognitive kinsfolk the aches, itches, thrills, twinges, spasms and qualms of nausea. I turn now to beliefs and desires: why should we conceive these as states or processes?

Doing so is certainly not natural. I argued above that primitive people have no concept of the mind at all. They do not differentiate intellectual functions from sense perception; neither have they any general concept of thinking. They account for each other's behaviour in terms of objects of desire and belief, not in terms of belief and desire themselves. A primitive man thinks his mate goes to a tree in order to gather fruit, and refrains from gathering because there is a serpent there. He can tell an anthropologist what fruit and serpents are, but not what belief and desire are. Clearly if he does not think that there are such things as belief and desire at all, he cannot think they are states, processes or properties.

It may be thought that we are forced to regard beliefs and desires as states by grammar. The sentences 'He wants to go home' and 'He thinks that that dog has rabies' are grammatically similar to 'He is brown-skinned' and 'He is six feet from that dog'. If the second pair of sentences attribute states to the person referred to, so do the first.

Anyone with a serious interest in grammar will think the first two sentences quite different from the second, for they contain verbs of wanting and thinking, and these, like the explanatory conjunctions, introduce special grammatical constructions. A philosopher of logic may define a predicate-expression as what is

[59]

left of a sentence when we have removed the definitely referring expressions, and define a property or state as that, whatever it may be, which is expressed by a predicate-expression. But these definitions will not be helpful to grammarians, and they do not advance a philosopher one inch in showing that a person's thinking something or wanting something is anything like an object's instantiating a physical property or standing in a spatial relation. The most we can say is that subject-predicate analysis probably encouraged Descartes to conceive beliefs and desires as properties of thinkers, rather as I shall be suggesting it has encouraged later philosophers to think that the deepest kind of explanation is physical.

Philosophers are led to conceive beliefs and desires on the model of physical states or processes by the use of two other models, the use of naturalistic painting as a model for thought, and sight as a model for our knowledge of what we are thinking. Naturalistic painting seems to cast a spell on them. Early Greek painting is severely stylised, and naturalism hardly got under way before the birth of Plato. Plato speaks of it in hyperbolical language: the painter is 'nothing short of a magician' (*Republic* 10. 602 d); his products are 'a kind of waking human dream' (*Sophist* 266 c). It has been suggested that what evokes this amazement is a kind of pointilliste technique: pictures that look a mess from near at hand but highly naturalistic from further off. This, however, would not explain Plato's saying that besides conceiving thinking as a kind of silent speech or writing in the soul we should imagine a painter 'who draws likenesses in the soul' [for] 'one in a way sees likenesses in the soul of the things that have been thought and said.' (*Philebus* 39 b–c.) It is significant that fullest use of pictures as a model for thoughts is made in the seventeenth century, which is the golden age of naturalism. Descartes, Locke and Leibniz were not only contemporaries of Peter de Hooch, but very familiar with the part of Europe in which his art flourished.

A picture is an expanse of canvas or paper, plaster or wood, coloured in a certain way; so if we use a picture as a model for a thought we conceive the thought as standing to the mind, or perhaps even to the thinker, as a pattern of colours to a canvas. Thinking is like the process of colouring, or perhaps like the expanse's state of being coloured.

What draws us to this model? The fact that when we look at a naturalistic painting it is just as if we were looking at the depicted scene. Stationed before Botticelli's 'Birth of Venus' we can see just what a beautiful goddess, standing on a shell, would look like. The painted panel does not come between us and the goddess: Venus on her shell seems to be directly presented to our mind. But of course, there is no goddess in the Uffizi: just painted panels and innumerable tourists. It is this vivid, direct presentation to consciousness of something that is not physically present, which makes pictures seem so perfect a model for beliefs and desires. Wanting an apple or believing there is an adder in the grass is just like seeing a picture of an apple or an adder, except that there is no picture there. In both cases we gaze with non-physical eyes on non-physical realities.

The only way to break the spell pictures cast, is to see that we are misunderstanding our experience of them. Interpreting Botticelli's masterpiece is not seeing a second, mental likeness of a goddess; it is realising what real object would affect your eyes as the picture does. No doubt the universe contains or might contain other things besides goddesses that, under some viewing conditions or other, would have the same effect. But they are not things that come into your head when you look at the picture. Looking at a picture you try to think of something painters in our society depict that would affect us as that picture does; or rather as some part of it does. Having thought 'A goddess a few yards off would affect me like this' you then reconstruct a scene that would have the effect of the whole picture; and you proceed to discern more and more about the things it would contain. You see what sort of hair a goddess that affected us like this would have, where her hands would be and what they would look like. Realising this is an intelligent use of sight. It is complementary to the painter's telling, by looking at a real lady across the room, what colours and shapes he must use to produce an naturalistic painting of her. In our picture-saturated society we all have the painter's ability to some extent. Distant mountains look blue to us, railway lines seem to converge, etc.

Some philosophers have thought that the convergence of the rails or the blue colour of the mountains is directly presented to the mind. They have construed our certainty about how the distant physical objects look as a certainty that certain non-physical objects *are* blue or converging, and think they have discovered a class of non-physical objects known only to philosophers, which they call 'sense-data'. It is a safe rule that whenever we think we have found a class of things that can be investigated only by philosophers – propositions and universals are further examples – we have made a mistake. Our certainty about how the distant objects look is a certainty that blue paint on canvas and converging lines would do the naturalistic painter's trick. The error that interpreting a picture is being presented with a non-physical replica of the depicted scene is the converse of the sense-datum error. There we see something three-dimensional, and know what a two-dimensional physical likeness would be like; when we look at a picture we see something two-dimensional and know what a three-dimensional reality would be like.

If we conceive thoughts on the model of pictures, it will be natural to conceive our knowledge of our thoughts on the model of sight. We often know quite well what we believe or desire; and we know this neither by hearsay nor by inference, neither by listening to our analysts as Freud recommends, nor by observing what we do and working out what we must have believed and desired in order to do that, as Gilbert Ryle preferred. We know what a picture depicts by looking at it. Locke suggests that we know the contents of our minds by a capacity which, 'though it be not sense, yet it is very like it, and might properly enough be called "internal sense".' (*Essay* 2.1.4.) Philosophers today are shy of the expression 'internal sense', but they still model Eve's knowledge that she wants an apple, but sees there is a snake present, on her knowledge that the snake is present and the apple is ripe. Once we conceive our ordinary consciousness of our thoughts on the model of sense-perception, even if we do not conceive the thoughts themselves as non-physical pictures we are pretty well bound to conceive them as states or properties of the thinker.

This way of conceiving them will seem appropriate only so long as we assume that our thoughts are somehow there independently of being known; that our knowledge no more determines the content of desires and beliefs than it determines the spatial relations of serpents and the ripeness of fruit. This assumption needs only to be formulated to be doubted. We believed what we believed in the past independently of what we now think we believed; but our knowledge of our past beliefs and desires, at least when they were of serious practical importance, is often inferential. When Clarissa is dead Lovelace may come to know that he really did want to marry her. In a time of religious persecution a crumbling pillar of the church may recognise that he never really believed that the gospel narratives were true. But it is not like that with our present beliefs and desires. If while she is still alive Lovelace asks himself, 'Do I now want to marry Clarissa?' he arrives at an answer by considering her good and bad qualities and the advantages and disadvantages of the match. Arriving at the knowledge that he wants to marry her is having it come to be true of him that he does. Suppose similarly that you ask Ophelia whether she thinks that if interest rates come down, so will unemployment. If you had asked her whether Polonius thinks that, she might have said 'I don't know. I haven't asked him.' But if you say 'What do you think, Ophelia, about the unemployment in Denmark at the moment? Do you think that lowering interest rates would bring it down?' she will not say 'I don't know. I haven't asked myself' – unless 'I haven't asked myself' means 'I haven't tried to form an opinion'. The question 'Do you think that p' (where p stands for any proposition: 'Do you think that smoking causes cancer?' or 'Do you think that all foreigners are shifty?' or what you will) is the question 'Is it, in your opinion, the case that p?', and you answer it by considering reasons for and against the proposition that p. Here too, discovering that

[63]

one thinks something is coming, after consideration, to think it. I know straight off that I think something is the case if I know for sure that it is. I know that I believe the cat is on the mat if I can see it there. Beliefs can be held unconsciously, but in general, coming to know that I have a belief is not discovering but confirming it. Our knowledge of our beliefs and desires is, in the scholastic phrase, a cause of what it knows.

I have now argued against several reasons for conceiving beliefs and desires as states; but how else, it may be asked, are we to conceive them? Since it is true to say that Othello believes Desdemona loves Cassio if, for the reason that she loves Cassio, he kills her, we may say that in general, believing that something is the case is being active or inactive *for the reason that* it is the case. Equally desiring that something should occur is being active or inactive *in order that* it should. The question then, is: 'How should we conceive doing something for a reason or purpose?' And the answer is: there is no special way. Doing something for a reason or purpose is not in itself different from doing it for no reason or purpose. Unfortunately, philosophers find it very difficult to come to terms with this answer. Let me try to explain why.

A first reaction to my analysis of belief is that it is obviously flawed. True enough, if Othello kills Desdemona for the reason that she loves Cassio, he must believe she loves Cassio. But his believing this is a precondition of his killing her for the reason that she loves Cassio; it cannot be constituted by his so acting. To this I have a double reply. First, if the belief that p is a precondition of action for the reason that p, what part does it play in that action? If none at all, why should it be a precondition? Surely it will have to play a causal part. Anyone who says 'Othello cannot kill Desdemona for the reason that she loves Cassio unless he already believes she does' is consciously or unconsciously considering the belief as a kind of cause of the action. But if beliefs are causes, physicalism follows at once. Anyone who wants to avoid physicalism must refrain from making beliefs and desires causes of action.

This is an *ad hominem* reply to the objection, powerless against an objector who is prepared to accept physicalism. A second, more general reply is this. In the statement 'If Othello kills Desdemona for the reason that she loves Cassio, he must believe she does' the 'must' should be understood as expressing logical necessity. The whole utterance is like 'If that woman has never been married, she must be a spinster.' Being a spinster is not a precondition of not being married. We can define a spinster as a woman who has never been married, and hence, if we like, argue that some famous courtesan is a spinster on the ground that she was never married. Equally, we can define belief in terms of acting for reasons, and then argue that a man did have a certain belief on the ground that some action of his must be explained by a certain reason. Since the difference between logical and causal necessity is more elusive than it sounds, let me take another example: 'I am older than you because I was born in April and you were born in August.' Being born before someone is not a cause of being older; it is what it is to be older. Likewise, believing something is not a cause of acting for the reason that the thing is true; it is what it is to act for that reason.

Next, physicalists usually start with the idea that believing and desiring are propositional attitudes. Propositions, in this context, are conceived on the model of naturalistic pictures, and the attitudes of believing and desiring are modelled either on bodily sensations (so Russell in *The Analysis of Mind*[10]) or on the bodily attitudes we may strike in a picture gallery in front of a picture we find realistic or fanciful, attractive or repulsive. The accounts of belief and desire I have just proposed may seem even more physicalist than these. To be precise, they may seem like behaviourism. 'Behaviourism' is the name given to the theory that there is no more to thinking than behaving – that is, acting and remaining inactive – in various ways. Is that not what I am saying? It is not. It would be behaviourism to say 'Believing that *p* is doing what it would in fact be good or reasonable to do if *p*.' I am saying not that, but 'Believing that *p* is doing things *for the reason that p*.' My analysis contains the connective 'for the reason that'. We shall see (in the last two pages of this chapter) that physicalists require such connectives to be eliminable. On my analysis, understanding a belief or desire is irreducibly teleological understanding, understanding action or inaction as being for a reason or purpose. It is essential to physicalism to reject understanding that cannot be reduced to causal.

When we are not doing philosophy we have no difficulty in understanding the behaviour of people around us teleologically. We also have a fair grasp of what that understanding consists in. It is never wholly detached, but always involves some willingness or unwillingness to intervene; usually it involves sympathy but sometimes antipathy. The Trojan Elders say 'We can understand Paris's plunging his country into war in order to live with Helen', and so far as it goes, that is an expression of approval; they say it only if they think it worthwhile to start a war for a lady who so marvellously resembles the immortal gods. 'I cannot understand his killing his sister for the reason that she wants to marry a commoner' expresses disapproval; it expresses that judgement that a sister's real or supposed desire to marry someone socially inferior does not justify the sort of behaviour we see in *The Duchess of Malfy*. Similarly, 'I cannot understand his taking off for Tahiti in spite of the fact that he had a family of young children in France' expresses the judgement that having a family in one part of the world makes it bad to take off for another. Thinking that a person is acting for a reason or purpose, indeed, involves two kinds of judgement. If I think that Othello is smothering Desdemona for the reason that she loves Cassio I must consider both whether she really does and whether, if she does, that makes it right to smother her. If the answer to either question is 'No', it is part of believing that Othello really is acting for this reason to try to stop him – unless, like Iago, I hate him, in which case I shall want to prevent anyone else from stopping him, and egg him on. Similarly, believing that you are going to London to see the Queen involves considering both whether it is worthwhile to make such a journey just in order to see her, and also whether seeing her can be achieved by going to London.

[66]

This is a conspicuous difference between teleological and causal understanding. If I really believed that Othello's killing Desdemona was caused by the belief that she loved Cassio, my judgement that he killed her because he believed she loved Cassio would no more involve evaluating his action than my later judgement that he is bleeding because he has stabbed himself involves evaluating his haemorrhage. When we think that a vessel shattered because a picture fell on it we need consider neither whether the picture depicted a real scene, nor whether its fall justified the shattering (though perhaps if we are to think about the matter at all the shattering must have some practical significance for us). It is possible to *say* that an agent acted for a reason or purpose without any apparent concern for the agent or any judgement on the truth of the belief, the practicality of the objective, or the rationality of the action. That is likeliest to happen if we are talking of an agent far removed from us in time or space. But then we are probably using words without really holding the beliefs they express. It may be enough to say what is commonly believed, or to exhibit the action as predictable or usual without caring whether it is rational or mechanical. But if we are genuinely explaining the action and yet have no involvement with the agent, then consciously or unconsciously we are taking a physicalist view of beliefs and desires, and thinking of the agent as a mechanism.

In practice we know it is a practical matter to understand someone else's, or our own, thought processes. But when we do philosophy the phrase 'understanding mental processes' acquires a new, theoretical meaning. We want to understand how people think – not what it is that they believe or want, but what they do in believing and wanting these things. Locke says that 'What perception is' – and he uses 'perception' for what 'is by some called thinking in general' – 'everyone will know better by reflection on what he does himself when he sees, hears, feels, etc., or thinks, than by any discourse of mine' (*Essay* 2.9.1–2); and he urges his reader to 'reflect on what he himself does when he wills' (*Essay* 2.21.15); Locke does exactly what Wittgenstein says: he supposes that there are *processes* of perceiving, 'willing' and thinking in general, in the way there are processes of sweating, walking and digesting. This forces him to a certain view of what it is to understand thinking, or even to have a conception of it. Just as we have an idea of digesting, walking or sweating when we know what we do to digest food, walk or sweat, so to have an idea of thinking is to know what we do when we think, perceive or 'will'. As understanding a physical process is knowing by what action of what upon what the result of that process is produced, so understanding belief or desire would be knowing by what action of what upon what we believe or desire something. Locke thinks we actually see this by 'internal sense'. Even if we reject that idea we imagine that there must be a process by which we come to believe and desire, and not the familiar process of reasoning, comparing, sifting evidence, etc., – a process like the process by which we sweat or digest food except that it has still to be discovered. Physicalists believe it is an occult physical process. Those who reject physicalism but retain the idea that believing and desiring are processes or states may think it is an occult non-physical process. But that is impossible. The notion of a process which we use when we speak of the process of digesting or perspiring is a physical notion.

There is a Rylean or Wittgensteinian strategy for seeing that it is nonsense to ask how we think. First, we ask ourselves how to bring about some specified outcome, say how to make glass, or how to get middle c out of a tenor recorder. The answer will be a process, heating sand, stopping certain holes or what not. We then ask how to make glass on purpose, or how to play middle c intelligently. We can explain the difference between doing something on purpose and doing it for no purpose, accidentally, but the difference does not lie in what is done: the hypothesis is that the same thing may be done accidentally or on purpose. If I ask how to make glass I am asking for a procedure or rule, by following which I shall finish up with some glass. If I make glass on purpose I am probably following such a rule, whereas if I make it accidentally I am not. Perhaps the rule is that I should heat sand to a certain temperature.

Consider then the question: 'What must I do if my heating of the sand is to be following the rule?' It will be following the rule if I heat the sand because the rule prescribes this. But while there is a difference between heating sand to the prescribed temperature in ignorance of the rule and doing do because the rule prescribes, the difference cannot be that in the latter case, besides heating the sand, I do something else. The rule does not prescribe anything further, and if it did, following the rule would be not merely doing this further thing but doing it because it too is prescribed. Similarly, we can explain the difference between acting intelligently and acting stupidly – probably in terms of reasons; playing middle c stupidly is playing it for no reason or when there is a good reason for not playing it, say if it is not in the score, or someone has told me not to play it. But again, the difference between doing something for a reason and doing it for no reason cannot be a difference in what I do. Or consider the difference between kissing someone on the stage as part of a play, and kissing the same person out of real affection: the process of kissing can surely be the same in both cases.

By this strategy we may convince ourselves that there can be no process by which we act for a reason or purpose, and no conception of bringing something about for a reason or purpose distinct from the conception of how to bring it about. If, therefore, belief and desire are what I say, there is nothing we do to believe or desire, and no explaining or understanding of them as there is of physical processes and states.

Perhaps it will be said that in this way we can stop people from asking certain questions about thought, but we do not thereby silence the physicalist. He or she can still say that every bodily movement, including every movement of tongue and pen, has a physical explanation. Of course, if the physicalist says simply that, people may reply 'So what?' and he or she may have to mention thought to get a rise out them. But I have been arguing that belief in mental states makes people physicalists, not that it is the only root of physicalism. Physicalists usually hold a theory of causation according to which later physical events are rendered necessary by earlier, and it is a law of nature that the earlier events should have these successors and that the universe should go on for year after year. They also tend to assume (perhaps because the Greek word *phusis* is translated by the Latin *natura* and the English 'nature') that the physical is coextensive with the natural, so that if what is psychological is not physical, it can only be supernatural. These ideas I shall not criticise in the present chapter. But independently of them, one reason why many philosophers feel that the real explanation of human behaviour must be physical is this. They believe that genuine explanation runs from the small to the large. What has components depends for its existence on the existence of these components, and whatever explains their movements and changes is the real explanation of the behaviour of the larger whole they compose. This idea about explanation is closely related to the idea that belief and desire should be conceived on the model of physical properties, so I shall conclude by examining it.

It can be applied to human beings in two ways: as individuals or as members of society. We individuals consist of cells, molecules, atoms, subatomic particles. So we can say without more ado that the real explanation of all our behaviour lies in whatever explains the behaviour of our subatomic particles. And what is that? According to classic physical atomism, the behaviour of any basic particle is determined by its intrinsic physical properties (including momentum), its spatial relations to other particles and their intrinsic properties.

But even today people feel that introspection gives them overwhelming evidence that they have thoughts and feelings, and cannot believe that these psychological phenomena have no genuine reality or explanatory power. Nineteenth-century 'pioneers of psychological theory' thought of their 'scientific mission' as that, not of doing away with the psychological, but

> . . . of duplicating for the world of mind what physicists had done for the world of matter. They looked for mental counterparts to

[70]

the forces in terms of which dynamic explanations were given of the movements of bodies. Which introspectible phenomena would do for purposive human conduct what pressure, impact, friction and attraction do for the accelerations and decelerations of physical objects? Desire and aversion, pleasure and pain seemed admirably qualified to play the required parts.[11]

Desire and aversion were conceived as states of human beings in the way velocity or momentum is a state of a physical body, and beliefs, perceptions etc., as intrinsic properties like a body's shape or texture.

This led to a kind of social atomism, distinct from but analogous to physical atomism. Mill says:

> The laws of the phenomena of society are, and can be, nothing but the laws of the actions and passions of human beings united together in the social state. Men, however, in a state of society, are still men; their actions and passions are obedient to the laws of individual human nature. Men are not, when brought together, converted into another kind of substance, with different properties . . . Human beings in society have no properties but those which are derived from, and may be resolved into, the laws of the nature of the individual man. In social phenomena, the Composition of Causes is the universal law. (*A System of Logic*, 6.7.1)

That is:

> The effect produced, in social phenomena, by any complex set of circumstances, amounts precisely to the sum of the effects of the circumstances taken singly. (Ibid., 6.9.1)

What does Mill mean by 'the laws of individual human nature'? That can be gathered from an earlier essay; there are, he says

> . . . laws or properties of human nature which appertain to man as a mere individual, and do not presuppose, as a necessary

[71]

condition, the existence of other individuals except, perhaps, as
mere instruments or means.[12]

To understand a human atom's behaviour as resulting from the laws
of individual human nature, we must understand the atom as acting
to secure benefits and avoid evils it can experience as an isolated
individual independent of any other sentient or intelligent being.

We experience bodily sensations as isolated individuals, and
some actions can certainly be explained as efforts to obtain pleasant sensations or to avoid pain. But sometimes we act in order that
someone else may avoid pain or loss; here the goal does apparently
presuppose the existence of another sentient being, not just as a
means, but as something to be benefited for its own sake.
Sometimes we act to discharge what our society considers a duty,
or refrain from doing something because doing it is considered
evil. On the face of it, to understand behaviour like this we must
consider the society, the whole, to which the agent belongs.
'However complex the phenomena,' says Mill, 'all their sequences
and coexistences result from the laws of the separate elements' (*A
System of Logic*, 6.9.1). To bring altruism and duty under this principle we must postulate desires to act dutifully and to benefit others
which we experience as individuals in the same sort of way as
hunger or sexual excitation. We must model aiming at the common
good or the good of other individuals on having bodily sensations
– which, if my earlier argument is sound, actually are bodily states.

Mill says explicitly that explanation in the social sciences should
be like explanation in physics. But we can reach a similar position
by striving to imitate not the physicist but the logician. Logic deals
with propositions, where by a 'proposition' is meant something
that is true or false. Whether truth and falsity attach primarily to
sentences, to utterances or to non-physical representations,
expressed in utterances, of possible states of affairs, is an important
question in the philosophy of language but not in logic. What is
important in logic is whether the truth of a proposition is determined by the truth or falsity of some other proposition or

propositions. If not, for logical purposes it counts as simple. 'The cat is black', 'The mat is white', and 'The cat is on the mat', at least at first sight, are simple. Propositions the truth of which is determined by other propositions are 'The cat *is not* black' (true if 'The cat is black' is false), 'The cat is black *and* the mat is white', '*If* the cat is black, this is not a hair from it'. These are technically known as 'truthfunctions' of the simple propositions on which their truth depends, and connectives that express truthfunctions like 'if' and 'and' are called 'truthfunctional'.

Propositions assigning physical properties and spatial relations to objects seem to be simple. A number of philosophers in the first half of the century, notably Russell, Carnap and the young Wittgenstein cherished the hope that complex natural phenomena might be adequately described in propositions which are truthfunctions of simple propositions of this kind, and that we should give the true, basic explanation of a complex phenomenon, whether physical or psychological, by asserting the true simple propositions which make the complex proposition describing it true.

The requirement that any complex proposition should be a truthfunction of simple propositions ensures that in formal logic, truth passes from the small to the large. It also seems to rule out the treatment of belief and desire which I advocate. For the conjunctions 'for the reason that' and 'in order that' are not truthfunctional; so when we use them, either we do not put forward genuine propositions at all, or the propositions we put forward are simple and atomic, like those assigning properties to objects. I suspect that those today who feel that physicalism must be true because explanation moves from the small to the large, however unconsciously, are modelling all explanation on explanation in logic and mathematics, and accepting the requirement of truthfunctionality. A basic teleological explanation might explain an action by an object's having or acquiring a property. It would present this as what rendered the action to be explained necessary, or what accounts for it as a reason or objective. But they do not accept this as an explanation because it does not conform to the logical paradigm.

If this is really why they espouse physicalism, they are confused. For the 'because' in 'The moon became dim because the earth came between it and the sun' is no more truthfunctional than 'in order that' in 'The guard ran forward in order that he might come between the president and the assassin.' The requirement of truth-functionality does away with physical necessity no less than moral; it does away with every kind except logical necessity; and that, unsurprisingly, results not in physicalism but the kind of logicism dreamed of by Descartes and Spinoza.

FIVE

Of Our Own Free Will

When Edward Dodson was asked, rather pressingly, to spend a week with his old friend Ursula Witherington, he thought it a nice idea. Oxford in mid-vacation was hot and crowded with tourists; philosophy, for the moment, seemed unresponsive to his wooing; and Miss Witherington, besides living in charming country and having a good cellar, was offering him the company of a couple of young Polynesian cousins. He liked all young people and the prospect of meeting two beautiful, naive savages, unspoilt by European civilisation, attracted him strongly.

Mr Dodson's age entitled him to reduced train-fares, and although Oxford has always resisted being part of the railway network, a single change at Birmingham placed him on a train doing a bishop's move from Cornwall to Caithness, from which he could descend at Newcastle and get a taxi into the wilds. British trains have scattered through them tables for four which are slightly less uncomfortable than the banks of bus-seats that predominate. Mr Dodson found one occupied only (on the window side facing forwards) by a young girl with a sweet face and long, thick fair hair. She was not plugged into a tape-player with a loud, pounding beat: on the contrary, she was reading a studious book. Mr Dodson seated himself across from her in a diagonal position. No soon had he done so than he had to rise to let in a clergyman who had also joined the train at Birmingham. But the clergyman was small and

[75]

elderly and immersed himself at once in a dumpy prayer-book full of psalms. This and the cut of his clerical collar enabled Mr Dodson to place him as a quiet sort of Catholic priest.

Mr Dodson felt it safe to start on a slow-moving novel he had brought with him; there was a constant trickle of passengers past his table on the way to or from the buffet, but he paid no attention to them. All the males, however, noticed his female companion, and suddenly a very disagreeable event occurred. A large, bearded man turned out of his course and dropped into the seat opposite. Mr Dodson moved his legs unwillingly and gave the newcomer a sour look. Though far from young, the bearded man had a deep sunburn and wore light, casual clothes. You could see that he was in good bodily shape because he had nothing in his pockets; the things men usually carry in their pockets were doubtless in a sort of Persian carpet handbag he carried with him. For half a minute he sat motionless like bomb that was about to explode. Then he proceeded to address the sweet-faced girl.

'And how,' he asked, in deep, rumbling tones with an American accent, 'do you like Master David?'

'Master David?' she repeated politely but uncomprehendingly. She had a soft, friendly voice.

'I see you're reading his *Enquiries.*'

'Oh, this. I just thought of him as Hume.'

'Master David Hume of Edinburgh.' Mr Dodson could see the priest twitch at the dreaded name. 'Is he turning you into a Pyrrhonian?'

The girl looked at him with melting blue eyes. 'A pironian? What's that?'

'A sceptic. That's what he's arguing in that book, that we ought to be moderate sceptics.'

It was worse than Mr Dodson had feared. He had supposed the man was just an ageing California hippy; now it appeared he was a philosopher.

'Oh,' said the girl. 'Well, it's a bit confusing, isn't it? I mean, he writes in such a difficult way.'

[76]

'Let me see.' The American's large, brown hand clamped onto the book. Mr Dodson shuddered.

American: 'So, you're reading that bit about "Of Liberty and Necessity".'

Girl: I'm trying to.

American: And you find it confusing?

Girl: Well, he seems to be saying there's no difference between them.

American: What's wrong with that?

Girl: How can we do anything of our own free will, if everything's necessary?

American: Well, you see what he says here. 'By liberty we can only mean *a power of acting or not acting, according to the determinations of the will.*'

Girl: But what does that mean? What are the determinations of the will?

American: He tells you in the next sentence. 'If we choose to remain at rest, we may; if we choose to move, we also may.'

Girl: So that's what freedom of the will consists in, doing what you choose?

[Mr Dodson could see that the priest had abandoned his psalms and was following the conversation with mounting impatience, but the American had no fault to find with the girl's definition.]

American: That's right.

Girl: But then what does he mean by 'necessary'? There was something he said a few pages before that. [Riffling the pages and holding the book so that both can read.] 'A man who at noon leaves his purse full of gold on the pavement at Charing Cross, may as well expect it to fly away with a feather, as that he will find it untouched an hour later.'

American: 'Fly away *like* a feather, not *with* a feather.'

Girl: Oh yes. But what has the purse to do with it? Because a purse doesn't have free will.

American: No, but the people in Charing Cross have. I guess Charing Cross is a pretty busy part of London.

[77]

Girl [laughing]: Very busy.

American: Hume means that people are just as predictable as things. You can be just as sure, if you leave a pocket-book full of English pounds on the sidewalk, that someone will take it, as you can that it won't grow feathers and . . . [With a touch of irritation] Well, lets cut out the feathers. Look at this bag here [bringing out the Persian carpet]: if I hold it up and then let it go, you can predict it'll fall, and stuff will spill out of it. [Lets it fall with a crash on the table. Various objects spill out.] If you think it was necessary for it to move down, then the movements of the thief are just as necessary when he takes the pocket-book on the sidewalk.

Girl: No, because he *shouldn't* take it – unless he's going to hand it in to the police. I don't think people's movements are so predictable.

American: Watch and see.

[From the contents of the bag the American took a slim, gold ball-pen and a pad of yellow paper and, rapidly writing a few words, tore off the sheet, folded it and put it under the bag. He also gathered up an expensive lighter and the grandest cigar case Mr Dodson had seen for many years, and proceeded to light a green American cigar. As the smoke went snaking through the coach, everyone looked up in astonishment. A ticket inspector shot down the centre aisle.]

Ticket Inspector: I'm afraid this is non-smoking accommodation, Sir. May I see your ticket? [The American fished out of his bag something that looked like a passport from Ghengis Khan.]

Ticket Inspector [scrutinising it]: This is a First Class travel pass. [Gasp from the girl.]

American: So what?

Ticket Inspector: The First Class accommodation is at the rear of the train. You can smoke there.

American: But this is the part of the train where the philosophy is. I take it I can sit here if I like?

Ticket Inspector: Then I must ask you to extinguish that cigar.

American: How can I? There aren't any ashtrays.

[78]

Ticket Inspector: If you give it to me, Sir, I'll dispose of it.

American [handing it over]: I dare say.

[When the inspector had gone, the American took the yellow slip from under his bag, and passed it to the girl. She read aloud: 'In less than five minutes, a conductor will tell me to put out my cigar.' The American grinned a great mouthful of well cared for teeth. Mr Dodson felt he had some justification, but discreetly kept his eyes on *Hillingdon Hall*. Even the priest relaxed his frostiness for a moment.]

Girl: You certainly predicted that. Five minutes – it hardly took five seconds.

American: But was the guy acting of his own free will?

Girl: Yes, I suppose so. But I don't see how it was necessary. At least, it may have been necessary if he was going to do his job, but it wasn't necessary as if, well, something was pushing him like the wind when it blows something over. I mean, the necessity came from inside him, didn't it?

American: Right. I'll give you an argument to show that you really believe that when someone acts of their own free will, something is determining them from outside.

Girl: That I think that?

American: That's right.

Girl: Like the wind?

American: Just like the wind.

Girl: Tell me.

American: Insofar as we act of our own free will, what we do is determined by what we judge to be best.

Girl: Could you write it down for me please? You see, I've got an essay on Hume.

American: Sure. [Retrieves the yellow block and starts to write.] Say, don't you guys have vacations in Britain?

Girl: Yes, but I was supposed to hand this essay in before the end of term. I got an extension.

American [finishes writing and tears off the sheet]: There. Can you read that?

[79]

Girl [reading aloud, with appeals for confirmation at each step]:

1 Insofar as I act of my own free will, what I do is determined by what I judge to be best.

2 My judgement on what is best is determined by what I believe to be the case.

3 My beliefs about what is the case are determined by what I perceive.

4 What I perceive is determined by causal action on my sense-organs.

5 So insofar as I act of my own free will, what I do is determined by causal action on my sense-organs.

American: Do you buy it?

Girl: Well, it's very logical. I can see it all follows logically.

American: Are the premisses true?

Girl: Yes. Except that I don't think we always do what we think best. Sometimes we do, but sometimes we're rather silly, or, well, we do what we think we shouldn't. [The last words were said in a low voice, with a bashful look that was not without effect on the American. While he was calling his wits to order, she turned her eyes across the table to the priest.]

Girl: Don't we, Father? You *are* a priest, aren't you?

Priest [overjoyed to obtain at last a piece of the action]: We certainly do. And I may say that I do not agree that freedom of the will consists in doing what we please. That is freedom from constraint. Freedom of the will is something different. It is the freedom to choose the course we judge best, or to reject it. Animals act only out of necessity. They cannot help following their natural instincts. But human beings have reason. They can see where their real good lies, and they are free to pursue it or to turn away from it.

[The American thought that there were enough people in the conversation already, and was not pleased by this appeal to priestly authority. The heavy benevolence he had been beaming at the girl was switched off, and a hard competitive gaze was swivelled across the table.]

[80]

American: And turning away from it is what you would call 'sin'?

Priest: Sin is usually defined as offense against God. But you could also describe it as the free rejection of the good that God offers. And it is a condition of a man's committing a sin that he has full knowledge that what he is doing is wrong.

American: Are you saying that a sinner knows he is choosing the worse course?

Priest: Acting in ignorance is not a sin.

American: But if he knows it is the worse course, why does he choose it?

Girl: It's because her will is weak, isn't it?

Priest: That is correct. If your will is strong, you will always choose what your reason tells you is best.

American: If reason is capable of telling that. [Turning to girl.] What does your friend David Hume say about that?

Girl: Does he say something? I haven't got that far.

American: He says we distinguish good and evil by feeling, not by reason.

Priest: It doesn't make any difference whether you call it 'reason' or 'feeling' or 'conscience'. Everyone agrees that it is one thing to judge that a course is best, and another to do it; and to pass from judgement to action we need the faculty of will.

American: I'm not sure I do agree. You say the will is a power to translate thought into action.

Priest: Yes.

American: But see here, there couldn't be a power like that. The power to talk Spanish or to lift a sack of corn is right from the start the power to do it. You don't need a further power to exercise the powers you have. If you did, you'd need a further power to exercise that, and then a further power again, and you'd never get started.

[The girl became glassy eyed at this. The priest took his cue from her and smiled.]

Priest: I'm afraid that's too deep for me.'

American: Well, look at it like this. You say I can work out it would be best for me to do something, quit smoking, for example. So when some nice guy offers me a cigar, I know it would be best to say 'No thank you.' But because I'm weak willed, I don't say that.

Priest: That's what most people think, isn't it?

American: Just how weak is the damn thing? I mean, am I just unable to say 'No thank you'? Because if I can't do anything except take the cigar, I don't take it freely, according to you.

Priest: You might not have the strength now. But strength of will is like bodily strength. [The American looked scornfully at the priest's shrimplike physique.] We can develop it by practice. Just as every normal man is born with some bodily strength, and some people exercise and become athletes, and others neglect their fitness, so everyone is born with a basic minimum of will power, but if they don't use it in small things, then when a big temptation comes along they cannot resist.

American: So let's have a look at the early stages. When we're kids we know we've only got this minimum slice of will power, and we'd better build it up. Why do some people build it up, and others not? Is it because some have got more will power? Do we need some super will power to develop ordinary will power?

Girl: I think when someone offers you a cigar you could say 'No' if you tried a bit harder.

American: You mean I've got enough will power, I just have to use it?

Girl: I suppose so. You have to make an effort to use it.

American: An effort of will? But that's a second will, isn't it, which we need to use our first will when we think it would be best to use it. And maybe the second will is a bit weak. Not too weak, we don't want that, but so weak that it takes an effort by a third will to use it.

Priest: That's a very ingenious argument, and I'm afraid it's many years since I studied philosophy. But it seems to me that you're going back to Socrates's position, that when people do wrong it is not because they choose to do wrong, but because they are ignorant, and believe it right.

[82]

American: At the time of acting, anyhow.

Priest: In that case, how can you blame them? And if you do something difficult that you see is right, if you couldn't have done anything else, how can you be praised? It seems to me that the Socratic view makes nonsense of the ideas of guilt and merit.

American: If that's really true, and right now I'm not prepared to say it is, maybe we ought to think again about our ideas of guilt and merit. You're making the tail wag the dog, if you construct your philosophy of human action to protect the system you've already got of rewards and punishments.

Priest [to girl]: What do you think?

Girl: Oh, I don't think it's right to blame people. I mean, who are we to judge?

Priest: Well, here we are at Chesterfield. This is where I get out. A very interesting conversation. I don't often have the chance to talk to philosophers.

[The small priest departed with the air of one who is a good loser, and Mr Dodson wondered if the American would now return to his original seat, and restore the table to silence and leg room. But at that moment someone came along pushing a trolly. The American produced an impressive bundle of notes from the carpet bag and persuaded the girl to accept a quarter-bottle of wine and a sandwich. After some light conversation over this snack, in which he elicited the information that she had just finished her first year at the University of Newcastle upon Tyne, that she did not know the surnames of any of the faculty, but that she had a nice tutor called Richard, the American recalled her attention to the piece of yellow paper with his argument.]

American: So, in spite of the good Father's warnings, you're ready to take the first step, and agree that insofar as I act of my own free will, what I do is determined by what I think best.

Girl: Yes.

American: What about the rest of the argument.

Girl: That what I do is determined by things that affect my sense-organs?

[83]

American: Yes.

Girl: You mean sound waves and light?

American: Yes.

Girl: Well, it's very logical, but it doesn't feel like that.

American: No. It's like a computer: what you feel is the software, but what actually happens is determined by the hardware.

Girl: How do you mean?

American: Think of a pocket calculator. Suppose you tap in 11, then the multiplication sign, then 7, and then the equals sign: what'll it display?

Girl: I don't know. I'd have to do it and see.

American: But you can work it out in your head. You know what 11 times 7 is.

Girl: No, I'd do it on a calculator. It's better that way, because you don't make mistakes.

American: Don't you have the multiplication table in British schools?

Girl: What's the multiplication table?

[The American picked up his bag and poured out some contents onto the table. It reminded Mr Dodson of the famous bag carried by Mary Poppins. Out of a mound of credit cards, smoking equipment and little gold boxes which somehow looked as if they held substances more illegal than snuff, the American selected a slender but clearly extremely versatile calculator.]

American: When you multiply 11 by a single figure number, the product is the number that consists of that single figure twice over. So look. I tap in 11 and the multiplication sign and 7. What will the answer be?

Girl: Two sevens?

American: Press the equals sign and see what shows up.

Girl: Oh! It's done it! Seventy-seven.

American: What'll you get if you enter 11 x 6?

Girl: Sixty-six.

American: So you can predict what the calculator will show, using this rule. But the calculator doesn't use that rule – it doesn't

[84]

know anything about it. The buttons on the calculator show numbers in decimal notation, 1, 2, 3, 4 and so on. But any number that can be expressed like that can also be expressed in binary notation, in 0s and 1s. The calculator consists of parts that are in one or the other of just two states, what you could call 'off' or 'on'. When we enter a number, it gets translated into binary notation, and represented by states of the calculator's components. They interact according to physical laws, not rules for doing sums, and finally the result gets translated back into decimal figures in the display. Do you follow?

Girl: Yes, we did do that at school.

American: It's the same with the human brain. The things we see and hear, animals, trees, voices, melodies and so on, are like the decimal figures, and we calculate how people will behave in terms of them, using rules of prudence and morality. But the brain consists of neurons and each neuron either fires, and sends on an impulse along a nerve, or doesn't fire. Light rays act on the retina, which consists of nerve endings, and sound affects the inner ear which contains the ends of the auditory nerves. The neural impulses move through the brain, and either the neurons stop firing, or the impulses end by stimulating the motor system of nerves and muscles, and the hands or the legs or the tongue moves. And we translate that into movements in response to a bottle of wine or a violin sonata or a charging elephant. But the brain doesn't know anything about violins or elephants or pleasure or danger. The neurons fire according to physical laws.

Girl [eyes shining]: So, we're really the same as computers?

American: You could put it that way.

Girl: That's step 5, isn't it? 'Insofar as we act of our own free will, what we do is caused by things acting on our sense-organs.'

American: Yes.

Girl: It's a valid argument. But I wonder if everyone would agree. I wonder if someone who wasn't a philosopher, like . . .

[The girl's eyes turned meaningfully towards Mr Dodson. Mr Dodson certainly did not look like the popular stereotype of a

[85]

philosopher. His still plentiful silver hair was cut short, his clean-shaven, aquiline face looked like that of a slightly self-indulgent outdoor man of action, a soldier or explorer, and he was wearing a well cut summer suit of pale grey and a festive silk tie.]

American [not enthusiastic about roping in another party to the conversation]: I don't think the gentleman opposite is interested in Hume. He's reading a sporting novel by Surtees.

Girl: But he must have heard what we were saying.

Mr Dodson [not one to be boorish in a situation from which there is no escape]: I did hear some of it, and it was fascinating. Of course, I couldn't follow the last part, about the neurons.

Girl: Oh, you didn't have to, that was just an extra. But look at this clever argument that this philosopher, I think he must be a Professor . . .

American: Just call me Si.

Girl: That Si has written here. It shows how free will and necessity are the same thing.

Mr Dodson: Very good. Very neat.

Girl: But do you think it proves it?

Mr Dodson [examining the yellow paper]: I don't think I quite understand this fourth step, that what I perceive is determined by causal action on my sense-organs.

Girl: Well, that's rather scientific. It's talking about sound-waves and light.

Mr Dodson: A few years ago I had an opportunity to visit a tribe that lived in the forest up a tributary of the Amazon. Their culture was what we should class as Stone Age. When we went into the forest, there were just the same stimuli to my eyes and ears as to the Indians'. But they saw and heard an enormous amount more than I.

Girl [impressed]: Snakes and spiders? I suppose the Indians have much keener eyes and ears than we have.

Mr Dodson: Not necessarily.

Girl: But they use them more than we do.

Mr Dodson: Not that either. But you have to learn how to use your eyes and ears; and you learn to recognise specific things in specific circumstances. It's the same with tools and instruments. Nobody just learns to use a pen or a knife. They have to learn how to draw in ink with a pen or to write in a particular language; how to chop up vegetables with a knife or carve wooden images or fight. You can be good at Chinese calligraphy with a brush, but not just good at using a brush. An Indian learns how to pick out human beings and various kinds of edible creature in the forest; we learn to pick out human beings and various kinds of vehicle in city streets. And the Indians could see things I had no idea of, like the territory of a particular sort of animal, or the old women's part of a village.

Girl: And there are things you have an idea of that they hadn't.

Mr Dodson: Certainly. If I had snatched up the Chief in a helicopter, and set him down in a party in London for the launch of a book on economics, he would have had a completely different perception of his situation from a stockbroker, say, who had been to Eton or [with a bow to the American] Groton. So it seems to me that the sound waves and light particles play only a very small part in determining what we perceive.

American [accusingly]: You're using 'perceive' in a broad sense, to cover anything a philosopher would call 'the application of concepts'.

Mr Dodson [humbly]: Yes, I dare say I am.

American: You aren't distinguishing the fourth step of my argument from the third.

Mr Dodson: I'm sorry. I didn't see how you could draw a firm line between what I believe about how I'm situated at any moment, and what I perceive.

American: It's the line between your perceptual data, and what you believe on the basis of those data. For instance we could see that that little guy who was here was wearing black and we could see the shape of his hat; and from that we inferred that he was a priest.

Mr Dodson: An Indian from the Amazon might have had to infer

[87]

he was a priest, but personally I thought of him as a priest from the moment I set eyes of him.

Girl: It must have been an inference, but it was too quick for you to notice.

Mr Dodson: Ah.

American [magnanimously]: But we needn't insist on the difference between perception and belief, and you've made a good point, Sir, that perceptual recognition is an acquired skill. But that only strengthens the argument. For of course what we perceive cannot depend solely on what stimuli reach us. Otherwise something without a sensory system at all, like a bagel, might see and hear.

Mr Dodson: What is a bagel?

American [not heeding him]: If an organism is going to respond to a kind of predator or prey at all, it will have to be able to respond to it under different viewing conditions, by different lights, at different distances and angles. That requires a modification of the sensory system; additional structure must be built into it. To be able to spot a priest you must be able to respond to a particular range of colours and shapes, and probably movements of hand and face too. That takes time: a baby can't do it. But why is time needed, and why, in the end, can you do it while an Amazonian Indian can't, unless there's a physical structure being set up in the neural pathways of the brain?

Mr Dodson: Perhaps you are right, and I was misled by the comparison with a calculator. Calculators are produced by the million, and they all calculate in the same way, but if I understand you, when it comes to processing visual and auditory data, all people are different to a greater or less degree.

American: Yes.

Mr Dodson: But there's another matter that troubles me, unless it is the same matter in a different guise.

American: What's that.

Mr Dodson [to girl]: You mentioned snakes and spiders, and I noticed that Europeans when they first encounter South

American specimens often judge them to be larger than they really are.

Girl: That's because they're scared of them.

Mr Dodson: Exactly. On the other hand in spite of all the warnings they read, when English people go on holiday to Europe they bask in the sun as if there were no such thing as sunburn, let alone skin cancer.

Girl: That's because the sun feels so good after the English winter.

Mr Dodson: So people make wrong judgements about things, and especially about their harmfulness or harmlessness, because of feelings of fear and pleasure and so on? It's a question of fact, say, how many alligators there are in a pool, but our factual judgement can be distorted by our emotional state.

American: We know about that. It's called 'hot irrationality'.

Mr Dodson: And there are also our judgements about what other people know and don't know, or want and don't want. They're judgements about what is the case, not about what we ought to do?

American: Yes, they're liable to hot irrationality too.

Mr Dodson: If I'm angry with someone, I may think he knows he's inconveniencing me, when he doesn't, or that he's doing it on purpose, when he isn't.

Girl: That's why you're angry with him, because you think that.

Mr Dodson: But mightn't it be the other way? If I wasn't angry, I should see that he couldn't possibly know he was injuring me, and that he has no reason to be hostile to me? The same sort of thing happens with love, doesn't it?

Girl: That someone thinks you love them, when you've tried to tell them you don't? Or you think they won't mind if you're a bit unfaithful, when of course they will?

Mr Dodson: Precisely. How does that sort of thing fit into the pocket-calculator picture?

American: No problem. Emotional states are always supervenient on bodily states.

Mr Dodson: They're what?

[89]

American: Suppose you get mad or scared. You don't believe that might be the only change that takes place, and there isn't a change in your brain as well? Suppose that you and I see a beautiful Indian girl in your forest, and I get horny and you don't. Could that be the only difference between us, or would there have to be a physical difference too?

Mr Dodson [deeply embarrassed]: I think you'd really have to ask a doctor that.

American: And that's why we might make different estimates of the likely results of kissing her. [To girl] It's quite true that people with different feelings will have different beliefs about what is the case. But that's for the same reason that people with different concepts and capacities for perceptual recognition will. The real explanation lies in physical modifications of the nervous system.

Mr Dodson: But there's a difference. Being able to pick out a priest or an anaconda, that's a fairly permanent capacity. Emotional states come and go, and are thought to be to some extent under our control. We can resist fear or anger in a way we cannot resist a capacity to recognise tarantulas. Or if we *can* train ourselves to notice some sorts of thing and not others, that again reduces our resemblance to pocket calculators.

American: The similarity doesn't have to go beyond this, that just as we can interpret the display in the calculator as the correct solution to a mathematical problem, but it is actually the necessary consequence of our action on the calculator and the way it is constructed, so we can interpret human actions as a rational response to the agent's situation as she believes it to be, but they are in fact the inevitable result of the stimuli on a neural system such as hers is at the moment. But I'm afraid this is dull stuff, and we're keeping you from your friend Mr Jorrocks.

Mr Dodson [now roused]: No, I find your argument intriguing.

Girl: And you're convinced, now that Si's explained it?

Mr Dodson: I see what he's claiming in steps 3 and 4, but I'm still a little puzzled by step 2.

Girl: You don't agree that what we think we ought to do is determined by what we believe is the case?

Mr Dodson: That depends. When the Professor talks about what we believe to be the case – you don't mind me calling you 'the Professor' do you?

American: No.

Mr Dodson: You mean beliefs about the things around us at the time?

American: Yeah.

Mr Dodson: Well, I might see a lot of fish in the water, but that wouldn't determine whether I thought it a good idea to dive in and swim, if I didn't know what they were.

American: Of course not.

Mr Dodson: And even if someone told me they were piranhas, I still might think it all right to dive in, if I believed piranhas were harmless, like trout.

American: The belief that determines your judgement would be the general belief that piranhas are dangerous.

Mr Dodson: I think 'Piranhas tear swimmers to pieces; there are piranhas here; so it's best not to swim.'

Girl: That's very good. Can I write that down for my essay?

[The American passed her the carpet bag, and she wrote the reasoning on a yellow slip. She seemed to be one of those people who can write only if their head is on a level with the paper and they squint at it from the side. All they could see was her long fair hair, that fell over her face like a curtain and piled itself up in heaps on the table.]

Mr Dodson: All right. But suppose I believe a chap's been trifling with my sister's affections. I might do anything. I might just tell her not to be such a fool another time. But if I was Laertes I might want to murder the chap.

American: Laertes believes that a man has a duty to take vengeance on anyone who slights a woman in his family.

Mr Dodson: And you count that among the beliefs that determine his action?

American: Why not?

Mr Dodson [to girl]: What do you think?

Girl [reading aloud as she writes it down]: Laertes thinks: 'If anyone sights my sister, I ought to murder him; and Hamlet has sighted my sister' – it *is* Hamlet, isn't it?

American: 'Slighted', not 'sighted'.

Girl: So he thinks he ought to kill Hamlet. Yes, it's just the same as with the piranhas.

Mr Dodson: Not quite. Anybody that thought there were ferocious predators in a pool, any living organism even, would think it best to keep out. I make the judgement just as a sentient individual. But you have to belong to a special macho society to think that when someone sights your sister it's best to kill him. Laertes makes his judgement as a renaissance Dane.

American: What difference does that make?

Mr Dodson: Perhaps none. But . . . Mightn't Laertes think that Hamlet has insulted his sister, and also think that it's best to wreak vengeance on anyone who insults your sister, but still not think it's best to slay Hamlet?

Girl: Because he's tender hearted, you mean?

Mr Dodson: Because he's irrational. Perhaps we ought to add another belief. If Laertes is rational, he thinks this. 'If you believe that you ought to slay anyone who insults your sister, and you also believe that this fellow here has insulted your sister, then you ought to judge that you should slay this fellow here.'

Girl [writing desperately]: You mean all that's another belief? I'm not sure I've got it down correctly.

American: You needn't try, because if you do, our friend will get you to write down something worse. What he's just formulated isn't a premise in Laertes's reasoning; it's a rule of deductive inference.

Girl: How do you mean?

American: It says it's O.K. to go from the premisses to the conclusion. If you try to make that another premiss, you start on a regress.

[92]

Mr Dodson: I see. But couldn't the same be said of the principle that men have a duty to avenge insults to the women in their family? Surely Laertes's reasoning is really: 'Ophelia is my sister. Hamlet trifled with her affections. So I ought to slay him.' It's O.K. to go from the premisses to the conclusion in renaissance Denmark, and 'Renaissance Danes were under an obligation to avenge insults to their sisters' tells us that. But the reasoning might not be valid in twentieth-century California.

American: You're misled by the way people use the word 'valid' in ordinary conversation. Strictly speaking, reasoning is either valid or invalid. It can't be valid for one society and not for another.

Mr Dodson: But that's my difficulty. 'There are savage predators here so it's best to keep out' is valid for every sentient individual. But some things make a course seem good or bad only if one judges not as an individual but as member of a society with its own idiosyncratic life, enshrined in its own laws and customs.

American [patronisingly]: You're not using 'valid' correctly. It's never valid to go from a premiss saying what is the case to a conclusion saying what's right or wrong.

Girl: Isn't it?

American: But never mind about that. What this gentleman is missing out is that besides an instinct of self-preservation we have a gregarious instinct, an instinct to run with the herd, that's just as strong as the instinct to eat or shun pain.

Mr Dodson: You think that Laertes really wants to satisfy his herd instinct? Or he's afraid of being excluded, and he thinks he has to take vengeance to escape that? I'd imagined that when he thinks 'This lovely distraught girl is my sister,' slaying Hamlet seems to him an end in itself, apart from any consequences that may follow either from bringing it off or from failing to attempt it. You spoke of an instinct to shun pain. The same issue arises over that. You would perhaps say that pain is something we are averse to for its own sake, independently of consequences; we are so made that we abhor it.

American: I'd certainly say that.

Mr Dodson: I'd say something rather different. There are some states we avoid or try to get rid of as an end in itself. We use the word 'painful' to label these states, and saying 'Being burnt is painful' is equivalent to saying it is an object of aversion to us as sentient individuals. On your view, there's just one thing we dislike in itself, pain, and we dislike being burnt or frozen or cut because that causes pain. On the alternative view I am offering, we dislike being burnt, being cut and various other states for their own sake; we are aware of them from the start as conditions to be shunned; and that's what it means to say 'They hurt'.

Girl: It sounds very complicated. What has it got to do with duties?

Mr Dodson: The same problem arises. People sometimes do a thing because it's a duty, but what does that mean? Does Laertes just have one objective, to do his duty, and does he avenge insults to Ophelia as a sort of means to that? In that case all dutiful people will be rather similar, and perhaps a bit sanctimonious. Or do dutiful people in different societies have different ranges of objectives? When I say: 'In Denmark brothers have a duty to avenge insults to their sisters' am I saying that avenging insults to sisters is one of the things that are ends in themselves to Danes – ends to them not as sentient individuals but as members of Danish society?

Girl: I don't think you ought to take revenge, not like that. But what about kindness? That isn't a duty, I mean, if you have to do something it isn't being kind. And it isn't just a social thing, because we can be kind to animals, like butterflies or whales.

Mr Dodson: You're quite right. I wonder what kind of principle kindness is.

American: Don't you think we might act kindly because we have instincts of benevolence?

Mr Dodson: Do you mean being kind feels warm and cosy, whereas if we're cruel or inhumane we feel bad? Or do you mean we can desire the well being of someone else for its own sake?

Girl: I think we care for other people, and for whales and things, for their own sake.

[94]

Mr Dodson: So do I. But for that we don't need any further principles, on top of 'being frozen is painful' or 'looking after your parents in their old age is a duty.' When Edgar sees it's freezing outside, he thinks Lear had better come in, so he'd better try to induce him; and since Kent knows that Goneril and Regan are Lear's daughters, he thinks it right to urge them to look after him. The principle 'It is good to be kind' is a kind of super-rule that lets us use a circumstance which might determine someone else's judgement of what is best, to determine our own.

Girl: So step 2 is right after all?

Mr Dodson: Certainly what we judge best depends on what we think is the case. But sometimes we judge as egoists, each aiming at our own satisfaction; sometimes we judge as members of society; and sometimes we judge as altruists aiming at the good of others. And in each case our judgement is determined differently: the rules that take us from the circumstances to the best response are different in kind. Now, when we have a problem in arithmetic, the answer is determined by the numbers we start with in just one way, and people in the Professor's country know how to programme a machine to go through clickety-clicks that will correspond. It is hard to see how the clicks might be matched up with some of these ways of determining practical judgements, even taken singly, and much harder to see how they could be matched with all of them taken together.

American: Why is that?

Mr Dodson: In the first place, when we are really in a quandary, any course that we consider seriously will have some things to recommend it and some drawbacks. There'll be reasons for it and reasons against it. Some of them may be of the same kind. The course may be pleasant in some ways and unpleasant in others; or we may have conflicting duties. And there'll be reasons of different kinds: literature is full of conflicts between duty and humanity, social pressure and concern for individuals. The trouble is that we have no method of setting these pros and cons in the scales against one another in the way we can weigh flour and butter and raisins against each other at the grocer's. How is the inspired artist to decide between working on his picture while the light lasts and helping his wife with the baby?

American: That's called the 'problem of the incommensurability of goods'. We know about that.

Mr Dodson: And you have a solution?

American: We're making progress. There are various strategies.

Girl: When it's a really difficult case, I think what we decide is determined by the stars.

Mr Dodson and American [with one voice]: By the stars!

Girl: Well, the planets. [Modestly] I'm a Virgo, so I'd do something very simple. [Looking at Mr Dodson] I think you're a Libra. And Si's a bit of a Taurus.

Mr Dodson [gently but firmly]: But our whole discussion is running on the basis that, in one way or another, practical decisions are determined rationally.

American: The United States Government is spending billions of dollars a year on space research, and so far there's been nothing to suggest that the planets have any influence on human affairs whatever.

Mr Dodson: But another difficulty. Problems in arithmetic can be considered in isolation from one another. Practical problems don't occur in isolation. Suppose you're faced by a conflict between duty to family and duty to society. Then you must belong to a society that has its own broader or narrower conception of family, and its own traditions of policing; and its institutions will be in a particular state of health or disrepair. What weight you attach to the conflicting calls of duty must depend on this. Besides, you can't think every problem out from first principles. You have established patterns of behaviour. You can modify these gradually, you can act uncharacteristically on occasion; but you can't break violently with habits of successful practice. Did you ever read an essay by Sartre called *Existentialism and Humanism*?

American: Sure.

Mr Dodson: During the war Sartre had a student who wanted to know whether it would be better to go to England and join the Free French, or stay in France and look after his mother. Surely that would depend on what sort of person he was, what sort of son, how promising a soldier, and so forth.

American: That's called 'holism'. We know practical judgements are holistic.

Mr Dodson: It is handy to have a name, but it doesn't make practical calculation any more similar to mathematical. And there's a third difference. A mathematical problem has a unique answer.

American: Actually no. Sometimes there are a number of solutions that will all satisfy a set of equations.

Mr Dodson: In that case the answer is a disjunction. You set out the possible solutions and say any of them might be correct. But you cannot say they might all be correct. But with a practical problem several different solutions might all be right. Sartre's student cannot both join the Free French in England and look after his mother in France, but it might be good to go to England, and good to stay in France, and neither might be better than the other; whichever he did, he might be doing what was best.

Girl: Surely one would have to be better than the other, even if he didn't know which. A priest would say that God always knows which is best.

Mr Dodson: I dare say that the priest who was here just now would say that. But that's because he'd want to attribute to God the best kind of thinking there is, and priests, like philosophers, are taught to regard mathematical thinking as the paradigm of all intellectual activity.

Girl: What do you think is the best kind of thinking?

Mr Dodson: Since God, if he exists, created the world, perhaps we ought to model his thought on human creativity. Suppose Sartre and I are each writing a novel about a model student, and Sartre thinks it would be best for his student to go to England, and I think it would be best for mine to stay in France. Would one of us have to be wrong? For centuries painters have tried to paint the human figure, trees, the sea. We all agree that some of their attempts are worthless failures. We don't agree on an order of excellence in which the successful efforts can be ranked. Perhaps it's not in the nature of the case that there should be such an order. Some novelists are good at drawing characters and some aren't, and of the characters well drawn by great novelists, some are good people on the whole and some bad. But of good fictitious persons, does there have to be a best? The Greeks used to debate whether Achilles was better than Odysseus. We might argue about whether Ralph Nickleby is worse than Bill Sykes, or Uriah Heep than Dodson and Fogg. We can find it worthwhile to discuss these questions without believing that they really have an answer.

American: So what's your conclusion? That when we're trying to judge what's best for ourselves in a practical dilemma, whatever we decide is best really is best?

Mr Dodson: Within limits. If you take the work of an artist as your model instead of the work of a mathematician, you'll find your subject matter begins to have slightly different properties. We believe that if there are two trees, and we have sufficiently accurate measuring equipment, we'll always find, either that one is a bit taller than the other or (though we gib at this) that they are absolutely equal in height. But personalities and courses of action are less sharp-edged. They can be roughly equal in goodness, but beyond a certain point it makes no sense to say either that one is slightly better or that they are exactly equal.

American: It seems to be that you're getting back to the position of David Hume.

Mr Dodson: How so?

American: He said that for actions and personalities to be good is simply for them to give pleasure to people of wide experience who contemplate them disinterestedly.

Mr Dodson: Give pleasure? What did he mean by that?

American: Make you feel good.

[98]

Mr Dodson: Then I'm not taking up his position. People can argue rationally about what obligations should be attached to a given relationship, they defend or attack principles for resolving conflicts between duty and humanity. How they feel is less important than how cogent the reasons are that they produce. But you were trying to bring this lady round to an opinion her book had expressed on a different subject, an opinion about freedom and necessity. You're suggesting that our actions are free because they are determined rationally by what we take to be the case, but also necessary because they are determined causally by sensory stimuli.

American: That's right.

Mr Dodson: And the causal determination is the real determination, while the rational determination is just a sort of appearance.

American: I didn't say that.

Mr Dodson: Anyhow, to convince us that our actions might be determined in these two different ways, you produce your pocket calculator. What digits the calculator displays is determined mathematically by the numbers that are fed into it, but also determined causally by pressure on the buttons and electrical connections. And you suggest that there are causal processes in the brain which stand to the rational determination by circumstances as the electrical processes inside the calculator stand to the mathematical determination by numbers.

American: Surely that's what every sane man believes.

Mr Dodson: The flaw I find in this analogy is that rational determination is radically different from mathematical determination, as different, in fact, as mathematical determination is from causal.

American: That's what you say.

Mr Dodson: That's what I have *argued*. Practical reasoning takes completely different forms depending on whether we are reasoning as egoistic individuals, as members of a society, or as disinterested altruists aiming at the good of other individuals.

And the circumstances which determine rationally are, as you neatly put it, incommensurable, they determine holistically, and they determine less than uniquely. If that is so, the fact that something which is determined mathematically is also, at another level, determined causally, gives us no reason to think that something determined rationally may also be determined causally.

American: 'If that is so.' But I didn't buy that stuff about there being fancy kinds of validity in practical reasoning and moral principles being rules like *modus ponens*. The only kind of reasoning I count as valid is good, old-fashioned natural deduction.

Mr Dodson: A fine, heroic stance. But if I am right about how practical determination works, it will affect the last part of the argument on that piece of paper, and reduce the extent to which our perception of circumstances is causally determined. For I think you did buy the suggestion that our perceptions are influenced by our emotional state?

American: Yep.

Mr Dodson: And our emotional state is partly under our control? There are things we can do to reduce anger or fear or desire, if we think it best to do them?

American: Okay.

Mr Dodson: So if what we think it best to do is rationally determined, so, indirectly, is our perception of our situation.

American: But see here. Do you seriously believe that acting of our own free will is a kind of miracle, that we violate the laws of nature every time we do it?

Mr Dodson: Certainly not. I am convinced as you that all our behaviour has a natural explanation; every movement of our bodies is a natural effect of physical forces. At the same time, however, we have no alternative in practical life to regarding our behaviour as rationally determined. Your argument suggests that a rational explanation of an action somehow *implies* that it is causally determined. Of that I am not convinced.

Girl: Let me write that down. It would make a good ending to my essay. 'The argument implies that rational actions are causally determined. Of that I am not convinced.'

Mr Dodson [wincing slightly, and looking at his watch]: Do you know, my basic English instincts tell me it would be good to have some afternoon tea. [To girl] Can I get you a cup?

Girl: Yes, thank you.

Mr Dodson: What about you, Professor? Do you take tea?

American: Do British trains have decaff?

Mr Dodson: I'll ask. If not, will you allow me to use my practical judgement? When one is travelling in a foreign country I think it is often best to have whisky, whatever the time of day.

[Mr Dodson rose to go foraging, and the girl took the occasion to ask the American to let her out for a moment. As Mr Dodson moved towards the buffet he saw her heading towards a lavatory in the other direction. When he got back, carrying two large beakers of tea and two small bottles of whisky, she had not yet returned.]

Mr Dodson: Our companion is taking a while.

American: I expect she's waiting in line. You wait in line for everything in Britain.

Mr Dodson: I certainly had to, at the buffet.

American [appreciatively, tackling the whisky]: She's a lively girl. Though she shook me when she talked about the stars.

Mr Dodson: I thought that was a bit steep – that, and what she said about the multiplication table. You don't suppose she could have got off the train? It stopped at York when I was at the buffet.

American: No, she's going to Newcastle, remember.

Mr Dodson: Yes. [After a short pause] They don't teach philosophy at Newcastle.

American: But I know they've got a university there.

Mr Dodson: Yes, but they closed their philosophy department in 1989.

American: Why?

Mr Dodson: You'd have to ask them that.

American [seeing the way his mind is working]: But of course she's coming back. She's left her book here.

[101]

Mr Dodson: Ah, her book. [Reaching over for it] She's left it open at that passage she read out: 'A man who at noon leaves his purse full of gold on the pavement at Charing Cross . . . ' I hope your bag is intact.

American: [checking it feverishly and swearing atrociously]: She's got my lighter, my pen, my cigarette case, a roll of Swiss francs, a fortnight's supply of dope, and two gold snuffboxes that I paid thousands for.

SIX

Biblical Concepts of the Supernatural

'There are no peoples, however primitive, without religion and magic.' So Bronislaw Malinowski began a perceptive essay in the 1920s on 'Magic, science and religion'[1] and most people today would think the statement a truism. I shall be speaking of magic only in passing, but what do we mean by 'religion'?

That is a question which early students of sociology and anthropology, like C. P. Tiele (author of the *Encyclopedia Britannica* Ninth Edition (1886) article on 'Religions') did not think of raising. To them the notion of religion was completely unproblematic. As a result, Lester Ward could identify religion with a supposed instinct that draws people into society in the way hunger draws them to food:

> For want of a better name I have characterised this social instinct, or instinct of race safety, as religion, but not without clearly perceiving that it constitutes the primordial, undifferentiated plasm out of which have developed all the more important human institutions.[2]

Emile Durkheim was more wary. In the first chapters of *The Elementary Forms of the Religious Life* he acknowledges the need to look for a definition of religion. The one with which he eventually comes up has at least the merit of the unexpected. There is religion, he says, where and only where there is 'a bipartite division of the whole universe, known and knowable, into two classes which embrace all that exists, but which radically exclude each other', namely the sacred and the profane.[3] Malinowski's essay builds on this and refers to religion everything in the realm of the sacred which serves no ulterior purpose except that it 'establishes, fixes and enhances all valuable mental attitudes.'[4]

There is nothing to stop academics from using 'religion' to mean 'social instinct' or 'system of bipartite division' or 'method of preserving valuable mental states'; and if they do, they can say that every society has a religion without fear of contradiction. But non-academics who happily accept this statement generally take the word to be used in its normal, non-academic sense, and saying what that sense is, is not an easy task. 'Religion' as it is commonly used today has no equivalent in Greek, in Latin or, so far as I know, in the language of any society uninfluenced by the Bible. Even Eusebius, writing in the fourth century, has to make do with *theosebeia*, 'piety', *deisidaimonia*, 'superstition', and *threskeia*, 'worship'.

It may be thought that while there may be no unitary concept of religion, there is a group of religious concepts and people have a religion if they have gods, temples and priests. But the same difficulty arises about these things as about religion itself. What is a temple? We tend to apply the word to any impressive piece of architecture left behind by a vanished society, but how can we be sure that Stonehenge, for example, was a temple rather than an observatory, a calendar or a community centre? A temple is supposed to be dedicated to a god, but that is hardly true of Zen Buddhist temples, and in any case, how do we tell whether a word used by an alien society should be translated 'god'? We can be sure that people have the concept of a camel, and can bet that they have a word meaning 'camel', if we see them using camels. But gods are not observable like species of animal. Penelope in the *Odyssey* uses the word *theos* to address something as evanescent as a dream

(*Odyssey* 4. 831). Colin Turnbull in his study of the pygmies *The Forest People* says that their God is the forest[5]; but it is not *prima facie* likely that anyone should think that God is a forest or that a forest is God, and Turnbull takes no pains to satisfy his readers that the pygmies have any concept of God at all. How do we decide whether a role respected in an alien society is that of a priest rather than a physician, magistrate or social worker? W. J. Perry tells us that in central Sulawesi

> . . . men, except in rare instances, do not act as priests. That is
> reserved for women. Priestesses are not concerned with cults of
> gods: their functions are practical, for they are needed in
> ceremonies connected with illness, agriculture, funerals and
> house-building.[6]

Then why call them 'priestesses'? They sound more like rudimentary officials from the Ministry of Agriculture. Central Sulawesi is now Christian, but the main Christian denomination is the Salvation Army, something here regarded less as a religious denomination than as a social work organisation, and when in 1986 I visited some remote villages, unapproachable by wheeled vehicles, besides being still female the clergy seemed all to have jobs with the World Health Organisation.

'But at least,' it will be protested, 'primitive people all have a lively belief in the supernatural.' But how do we determine whether a belief which is current in an alien society but which we do not share is a belief in the supernatural? The word 'supernatural' should signify that which is above the natural. But what notion of the natural can we attribute to people that have never been influenced by Greek philosophy?

'Religion', 'god', 'priest', etc., are words we use as we do because we have certain paradigms. I suggest that these paradigms are all taken from the Old Testament. The religion of the Old Testament Jews (which was, of course, the religion of Christ and his disciples) is our paradigm of a religion. It contained a god, Jehovah, a temple and a priesthood, and they provide our paradigms of these things. It is easy to attribute religion to the ancient Greeks and Romans because they had temples, priests and gods rather similar to the Jewish ones. We know that from literature. We do not have any literature written by ancient Egyptians, Babylonians or Persians, but we can see their temples, and the Bible tells us they had gods and priests. Travelling round the world we can find things close enough to our paradigms in India, China, Japan and Mexico. Zeus is not really very similar to Jehovah, since he did not create the world but himself had a beginning, and he dictated no laws to human beings, though he may have had respect for some principles of justice; for all we know about the gods of Egypt and Babylon they may have been even less like Jehovah; still, Greek temples are much as we imagine Solomon's temple to have been, and Greek priests are clearly akin to Aaron and, indeed, to the clergy of Barchester.

Not only do we use Jewish paradigms in attributing religion to other peoples; we also follow Jewish practice. The Jews took it for granted that every nation with which they came into contact had a religion. But this assumption was unconscious; they did not have a word for religion, any more than did the Greeks or the Romans; and when we examine it, it becomes suspect.

The Greeks thought they ought to make offerings to gods and heroes, and clean up after profanations and sacrileges; they classed these activities along with paying special respect to parents and one or two other categories of person as pious or holy (*hosion*). There is certainly an overlap of piety and religion. But the Greeks regarded piety as one virtue among others, not necessarily higher or more important than courage, which preserves a society against its enemies, or temperance, which makes for civilisation.

Religion differs from piety in at least two ways. First, it is all-embracing. It is not in competition with courage or temperance because the virtues are subordinate to it; it decides what traits of character are good and what bad, and orders us to cultivate the former and rid ourselves of the latter. Its jurisdiction extends over

[106]

our relationships with other people, over what we do in the privacy of the closet, over the whole of our lives. Secondly, it is appropriated to societies in a way piety is not. Acute observers might discern differences between Spanish piety and English or Japanese as they might between Viking courage and French or Roman; but we do not speak readily of the Spaniards, Romans or Japanese as having different pieties as we do of their having different religions.

Hence, there is no natural rivalry between one society's piety and another's. The Greeks and Romans saw nothing threatening in the Jewish worship of Jehovah, and often admired Jewish devotion. Devotion is compatible with toleration and a plurality of cults within a single society. Eusebius reports how, when Dionysius, Bishop of Alexandria in the third century, said that Christians worshipped the one God who was the maker of everything, the Roman deputy prefect replied: 'And who is stopping you from worshipping this god too, if god he is, as well as the natural ones? You are commanded to worship gods, and gods of whom everyone has heard.' (*Ecclesiastical History* 7.11.9.) Religion, in contrast, perhaps because it claims to govern every part of life, aspires to being the unique religion of the nation or state, and tends to be intolerant. It is fairly obvious that these two features of religion are present in ancient Israel. The Mosaic law is issued by Jehovah but extends far beyond the details of his cult; the priestly order and, in later times, the High Priesthood claims authority over what goes on not just in the Temple but everywhere. The identity of the Jews as a people is bound up explicitly and indissolubly with the national god. And the piety of other peoples is spoken of in consistently abusive language. Whereas for a Greek visiting a foreign country, to make offerings to the local gods would be good manners, for a Jew it would be like adultery, a vile infidelity to the god to whom the nation is wedded (Hos 2.4; cf. Jer 3.1, etc.). Having this way of thinking is paradigmatic of what we count as having a religion or being religious. The Jews found it hard to conceive of any other way of thinking and attributed it to any other people with which they came into contact. To put it in our terms, Jews thought that religion is so important and so essential to the identity of a society that every other society must have it.

Although the notions of a god and a priest (I use the word to cover both male and female makers of offerings and interpreters of a god's will) are prominent and easily grasped elements in the notion of religion, to understand that notion we must understand their practical significance for people, and the fundamental element in the notion of a religion (which is what enables us to speak of atheists as having a religion) is that it is what matters more than anything else, that it is of supreme value both to the individual and to society. We owe the whole notion, this element and our paradigms of a god, a priest and a temple, to the Old Testament Jews.

How is the notion of a religion related to that of the supernatural? If what I have just said about religion is correct, though having a religion generally goes with believing in the existence of things, or desiring things, that we should count as supernatural, the two are not quite the same.

What *do* we count as supernatural? Gods, in the first place. But some gods are more supernatural than others. The forest of the pygmies, whether they think it is God or not, is not in reality supernatural, and one should ask for quite a lot of evidence before accepting that they conceive it as supernatural. The Homeric gods did not create anything, they were themselves the progeny of earlier gods, their thought, like ours, took place in their midriffs (*Iliad* 1. 608), they could be constrained (Ibid., 8. 10–27), and even wounded (Ibid., 5. 855–9), and the Greeks seem to have thought of them rather as a particularly exalted part of the natural order than as outside it. They are immortal, and we consider immortality a supernatural endowment, but the Greeks may have thought it natural for gods. Aristotle, at least, speaks of theology as a branch of zoology. But the Jews can hardly have thought of Jehovah as part of the natural order, since he created the whole of it. Also, as Greek thought matures, the gods intervene in the world less and less; in the later biblical books Jehovah's control of creation gets ever tighter. Jewish theology is supernaturalist.

[108]

We use 'the supernatural' to cover not only gods but ghosts and magic. But perhaps that is a loose way of speaking. In cultures where ghosts figure largely it is not clear that they are not thought of as part of the natural order: if they are different from ordinary living organisms, those paradigms of the natural, they often seem to belong to a lower, not to a higher realm. They dwell underground, their mental powers are diminished, their aims are unintellectual and often childish or malignant. Collingwood suggested that magic is skill in controlling people's emotions.[7] In that case it is no more supernatural than rhetoric. I think most people conceive it as a kind of causal agency science cannot explain at the moment. The magician is like an ordinary artisan in that he can bring about certain kinds of event, chiefly death, sickness, sexual desire and the transmutation of metals, but he does this by methods science gives us no reason to trust: by exploiting as yet undiscovered properties of natural products, eye of newt, toe of frog, etc., or by giving orders to agents not known to zoology such as demons. But there is no suggestion that magical effects are produced in a completely lawless way, and no reason why the laws which govern their production should not some day be discovered by methods we recognise as scientific, or why they should be significantly different from laws we already know. If they are not, then magic is not superior to the natural order.

Magic is not prominent in the Old Testament and neither are ghosts. Although the Jews did not try to explain natural phenomena, like everyone else they explained purposive behaviour, and their God acts for reasons and purposes. As their thought gains sophistication there is increasing emphasis on the difference between divine and human purposive agency. And within the field of the purposive they develop a notion of the supernatural which seems to be peculiar to them and which rests on a simple model.

What we call 'natural', as I said in Chapter Three, is best defined negatively, as what is not due to human efficiency or incompetence. Motor-cars, massacres and joint-stock companies are not natural phenomena; rocks, nettles, whales and earthquakes are. But much of what we see is nature modified by purposive intervention. Our ancestors turned virgin country into fields and gardens, and domesticated various useful plants and animals. Nowadays, almost all of our landscapes are man-made and pears, plums, chickens and horses are all the effect of skilful selective breeding. The Jewish idea is this. As nature in its wild state stands to orchards, vineyards and domestic animals, so these things and human intelligence and purpose generally stand to a supernatural order. God is a kind of gardener or farmer who raises, if not the whole of humanity, at least the Jews, to a higher level.

A classic statement of the idea is that made in Isaiah:

> My beloved had a vineyard on a fertile hillside. He dug it, cleared it of stones, and planted it with red grapes. In the middle he built a tower, he hewed a press there too. He expected it to yield fine grapes: wild grapes were all it yielded. (Is 5.1–2)

The image of the vine appears again and again in the Old Testament:

> You brought a vine out of Egypt, to plant it you drove out nations, you cleared a space for it, it took root and filled the whole country. (Ps 80.8–9)

And:

> Many shepherds have laid my vineyard waste, have trampled over my plot of land, the plot of land that was my joy. (Jer 12.10; cf. Ezek 17.5–6, Hos 10.1)

It is taken up, of course, in the New Testament (Mt 20.1–16; cf. 21.33–4, etc.). And Jeremiah, instead of a vine, speaks (Jer 11.15–16) of an olive, and the difference between the wild olive and the cultivated olive is used by Paul to compare the gentiles with the Jews (Rom 11.16–24).

Old Testament writers also use another model which to us

[110]

seems quite different but which was originally intended to express the same idea: they compare God not to a gardener but to a husband. Ezekiel says:

> At birth, the very day you were born, there was no one to cut your navel-string or wash you . . . You were exposed in the open fields in your own dirt . . . I saw you kicking on the ground in your blood as I was passing, and I said to you as you lay in your blood 'Live'; and I made you grow like the grass of the fields. You developed, you grew, you reached marriageable age . . . I bathed you in water, I washed the blood off you, I anointed you with oil . . . You were loaded with gold and silver and dressed in linen and silk and brocade . . . You grew more and more beautiful . . . The fame of your beauty spread through the nations, since it was perfect, because I had clothed you with my own splendour. (Ezek 16.4–14)

The idea expressed by both images is of a supernatural development of the natural. There is a natural basis that can be refined, but only by divine intervention that is in part gratuitous. God makes the first advances, initially to Abraham and then, through Moses, to his descendants; but he requires a positive response. In the Prophetic books (Is 2.1–4; 25.6–8) the vine and the bride symbolise primarily the Jewish people, and if they respond by keeping the Mosaic Law they can expect a peaceful and prosperous existence in their country. But from an early time the transformation was supposed to affect them not just as a nation but as individuals: they become 'a kingdom *of priests*, a *holy* nation' (Ex 19.5). People reading passages like the one from Ezekiel just quoted will naturally be led to apply them to themselves as individuals.

It is as individuals that Jews and Christians expect a life after death, if they expect it at all. Unlike the earliest literature of Greece and the East, the early books of the Old Testament are silent about any kind of existence for the dead. We first hear of such an existence in the Hellenistic period, and then it appears as a gift from God depending on moral achievement before death. 'The

King of the world will raise us up' say the heroic brothers in 2 Maccabees, '*since we die for his laws*' (2 Mac 7.9). And Wisdom assures us that '*The upright* live for ever: their recompense is with the Lord.' (Wis 5.15)

That life after death depends on an actual change in our nature becomes clearer in Paul.

> What is sown is a psychical body, what is raised is a spiritual body. There is a psychical body and there is a spiritual. It was written: 'The first man Adam came into being into a living soul.' The last Adam came into a life-giving spirit. First is not the spiritual but the psychical; then comes the spiritual . . . What I am saying is that flesh and blood cannot inherit the Kingdom of Heaven . . . This which is perishable must put on imperishability, this which is mortal must put on immortality. (1 Cor 15.44–54)

The idea of a supernatural transformation of the natural runs all through the New Testament. The difference from the Old Testament is that in the New Testament it is mediated by Christ: he is himself the bridegroom (Mt 9.15; Jn 3.29, etc.) and the son of the vineyard owner (Mt 21.33–9). The supernatural life of the virtuous after death is the life of Christ, communicated to them by baptism (Jn 3.5–6; Rom 6.3–5) and the Eucharist (Jn 6.32–58). It is by being baptised that the gentiles are grafted like wild olives and share in the richness of the cultivated olive (Rom 11.17; so, too, Col 3.1–2).

Christian writers acquainted with Greek philosophy are inclined to say that the human soul is immortal from the start. Athenagoras (flourishing 177) says we are made 'out of an immortal soul and a body' (*De Resurrectione Mortuorum* 13). But in Greek philosophy this idea goes with the doctrine of reincarnation, which both Christian and Jewish thinkers reject. They want each of us to have a brand new soul, not a predecessor's cast-off. One would expect the Judaeo-Christian position to be that in the womb we receive only a mortal soul, and this can become immortal after birth through baptism and fidelity to God's laws. This may, in fact, have been the view of Irenaeus. In *Contra Haereses* he picks up Paul's psychical-spiritual distinction:

> The breath of life is one thing, which makes men psychical, and the life-giving spirit is another, which makes them spiritual. (*Contra Haereses* 5.12.2)

Asked why there is evil-doing in the world, why God did not make people in such a way that they always do right, Irenaeus asks in reply:

> How will someone become God [that is, have a life after death in union with God] who is not yet a human being? How immortal, when in his mortal nature he has not obeyed his maker's rule? (Ibid., 4.39)

This conception of the supernatural seems to have no real parallel in Greek thought. In Greek mythology superhuman beings can educate or civilise us. Prometheus raised us from a brutish existence by teaching us arts (Aeschylus, *Prometheus* 442–71). When Nausicaa's maids have washed Odysseus, Athene

> . . . made him taller to look at and broader, and made his hair come curling down his head like hyacinth flowers. As an artist applies gold to silver, when he has been taught consummate craftsmanship by Hephaestus and Pallas Athene, and accomplishes delightful works, so she poured delightful beauty on his head and shoulders. (*Odyssey* 6. 229–35)

These favours, however, besides being mythical, hardly take us above the natural level. Plato has a vision of something superior to ordinary civilised life, and rather as the Jewish prophets use the relation of the wild to the domesticated to explain their conception of the supernatural, Plato uses that of an image to what it represents. Intellectual activity and the things it deals with stand to sense-perception and the things we perceive as those things stand

[113]

to pictures of them (*Republic* 6. 509–11; cf. 10. 596–7). But, by Plato's time, superhuman beings had ceased to intervene in human affairs, and his transformation is to be accomplished by academic (if not Academic) education. Similarly, the Romans thought that savage barbaric nations might be made peaceful and civilised (so Virgil, *Aeneid* 6. 852), but relied for this on upright Roman officials.

The Christian belief that human beings can share in the life of a god, perhaps by eating a sacrificial victim or drinking sacred wine, may at first seem to have parallels in many societies. We have that splendid compilation *The Golden Bough* or, if we want more of a primary source, Euripides's *Bacchae*. But whereas in Euripides being filled with the god results in drunkenness, sexual excess and destructive madness, in Christian thought it is connected with moral ideals of gentle philanthropy and humility which also seem peculiar to the biblical Jews. This connection not only confirms the uniqueness of Judaeo-Christian supernaturalism but also goes some way to explaining its lasting influence on European culture.

From an early time the Old Testament denounces oppressing the poor and weak (so Ex 23.6; Ps 10.9–11; 10.17; 22.24; 72.2–14; Prov 14.21; 16.19; 21.13; 22.22–3), Homer says 'All poor people come from Zeus' (*Odyssey* 14. 88; cf. 18. 485–7), but this idea is not developed in the classical period. It was thought by fifth-century Greeks that the gods would avenge ill treatment of suppliants (Aeschylus, *Supplices* 381–5), but it is hard to imagine a contemporary of Pericles saying: 'To oppress the poor insults the Creator; kindness to the needy honours the Creator.' (Prov 14.31; cf. 17.5; 19.17.) And the Old Testament is not content to preach beneficence in general terms. Wages should not be kept back (Lev 19.13); neither should a pledge an indigent debtor needs (Deut 24.10–12). Interest should not be charged on loans to the poor, at least if they are Jews (Lev 25.35–7 and often). Although there is no ban on slavery, Jews who become slaves through poverty should be manumitted in the seventh year (Ex 21.2; Deut 15.12). There should also be a remission of debts (Deut 15.12), and every fiftieth year a redistribution of land (Lev 25.8–10). In classical Greece these three things, remission of debts, distribution of land and freeing of slaves, were the dreaded programme of revolutionary mob-leaders; in Israel they were the code of the hierarchy. The whole Old Testament attitude towards the poor compares instructively with Cicero's in his *De Officiis*, a document which is a fair summary of Roman decency. Cicero goes deeply into the duty of vendors to reveal everything relevant to the fixing of a just price for their wares (*De Officiis* 3. 50–7), but says nothing about honesty between employers and wage-earners, and on liberality to the poor confines himself to the dictum: 'We should often give to suitable [*idonei*] people in need, but with discretion and moderation.' (Ibid., 2. 54.) The Old Testament precepts have none of these qualifications.

No doubt the Jews did not always live up to these precepts (cf. Jer 34.8–11). The influence of them, however, can be seen in Philo. Whereas Old Testament authors offer only practical counsels, Philo offers moral philosophy. In his *De Virtutibus* the qualities he analyses are *andreia, philanthropia, metanoia* and *eugeneia*. This list is completely different from those offered by Aristotle in his ethical treatises.[8] The only common member is *andreia* and whereas that word in Aristotle signifies primarily the military virtue of courage in battle, Philo uses it for endurance under hardship, sickness, old age, etc. *Eugeneia*, high birth, turns out not to be a virtue at all; Philo criticises the value conventionally set on it. *Metanoia*, regret for disrespect to God and for moral turpitude, combined with a determination to change, is not something to which either Platonists or Stoics are ever called. And there is nothing in Greek ethics quite corresponding to Philo's *philanthropia*. This is the settled state of character that disposes people to treat the poor and the weak as God's law enjoins. It involves a humane gentleness (*hemerotes*) (*De Virtutibus* 116), and extends beyond human beings to animals and even plants (Ibid., 140–9). Greek philosophers are not interested in our treatment of animals, and although Plato considers that a good character should have an admixture of gentleness

(*Republic* 3. 410 d–e), in itself he thinks it no more a virtue than its contrary, ferocity (*agriotes*), while the Stoics do not even mention it. The ideal Stoic character is more sublime than gentle.

Another quality more highly esteemed in Jewish than in Greco-Roman culture is humility (*tapeinotes*). 'Better to be humble with the poor than to share the booty of the proud' says Proverbs (Prov 16.19). According to Ben Sira, 'The greater you are, the more humbly you should behave; then you will find favour with the Lord.' (Sir 3.18; cf. Is 57.15.) The Greeks warned against arrogant pride, *hubris*, and expected the gods to punish it. But Plato is probably trying to formulate the view most Greeks held when he makes Hippias say:

> This is always and everywhere the finest thing for every man: to be rich, healthy and honoured by the Greeks, to reach old age and, having given a fine funeral to his parents, to receive a fine and showy burial from his descendants. (*Hippias Major* 291 d–e)

There could hardly be a more marked contrast with the famous words of Isaiah about the Servant:

> He was so inhumanly disfigured that he no longer looked like a man . . . He was despised, the lowest of men, a man of sorrows, familiar with suffering . . . Ill treated and afflicted, he never opened his mouth, like a lamb led to the slaughterhouse, like a sheep before the shearers . . . Forcibly, after sentence, he was taken . . . He was given a grave with the wicked. (Is 52.14–53.9)

Isaiah's first purpose was no doubt to describe the Jewish people rather than an individual, but the description was bound to influence individual ideals.

Old Testament passages like this and Psalm 22 were taken by Christians as prophecies of Christ, and the figure of Christ himself provides an ideal quite different from the wise man or philosopher idealised by the Greeks. Although later ages have compared Christ with Socrates, nobody in the first century would have considered

[116]

death by hemlock remotely akin to death by crucifixion. The social insignificance of Jesus of Nazareth and his horrible and humiliating end would have committed his followers to making a virtue of humility even if he had not consistently preached it by word (Mt 20.24–8, etc.) and example (Jn 13.4–15).

Mistrust of worldly success was accompanied among the first Christians by mistrust of secular learning. Paul almost certainly knew nothing of the academic education available at Athens (what could he know, having spent his life in Tarsus and Palestine?) but that did not stop him from saying:

> The words of the Cross are folly to those who are going to ruin; but to those who are being saved they are the power of God. For it is written 'I shall destroy the wisdom of the wise and set aside the understanding of the intelligent' [Is 29.14] . . . Since in the wisdom of God the world did not come to knowledge through wisdom, God decided to save those who have faith through the folly of the message . . . See how you were called, brothers: not many of you were wise according to the flesh, not many powerful or well born. But God chose the foolish of the world to shame the wise, and the weak to shame the strong . . . When I came to you it was in no abundance of argument or wisdom to announce the mystery of God . . . My argument and message lies not in the persuasive words of wisdom, but in the demonstrative power of the Spirit. (1 Cor 1.18–2.4)

What Paul calls 'wisdom' here is not the practical wisdom praised in the Old Testament but the academic learning familiar to the Corinthians. In disparaging it, however, he moves away from the Platonic and Stoic conception of the best life, in which academic intellectual activity is prominent. A follower of Paul could not agree with Plato that the intellect is the highest part of the human psyche in the enthusiastic way Philo does.

The Jews of the Old Testament, then, look forward to a raising of human nature by God to a higher level, and the first Christians hope to experience this transformation by obeying, imitating and

[117]

sharing in the life of Christ. But the Old Testament Jews expect that their coming closer to God will be manifested in concern for the poor and weak and a modest, gentle bearing. In the New Testament the preaching both of John the Baptist (Mk 1.1–4) and of the Apostles (Acts 2.14–38) starts with a call to *metanoia*. There will be no transformation of the natural without that. The Gospels connect the life of Christ with God's solicitude for the poor from the beginning. Before he is born, Luke (Lk 1.46–55) puts into his mother's mouth the splendid sequence of quotations we call 'the Magnificat':

> He has turned his gaze upon the humility of his slave-girl [1 Sam 1.11] . . . He has thrown down the powerful from their thrones, [Job 12.19] and raised up the humble [Ps 113.7]; he has filled the hungry with good things [Ps 107.9], and sent the rich away empty.

Christ's first sermon is on the text of Isaiah 61.1:

> He has anointed me to bring good news to beggars [*ptochoi*], to announce release for prisoners, sight for the blind. (Lk 4.18)

The example he sets is above all one of the Philonian virtues of endurance and philanthropy. And the life by sharing in which Christians are to be united with God after death is the life that ended on the Cross (Phil 2.7–9, etc.).

An existence above the natural is inextricably entwined, in the Judaeo-Christian tradition, with a willingness to go beyond natural obligations to serve others and endure mortifications.

SEVEN

Philosophy and the Supernatural

Fear of the supernatural is not confined to primitive people; it extends to twentieth-century philosophers of a physicalist complexion. Colin McGinn tells us:

> We do not want to acknowledge radical emergence of the conscious with respect to the cerebral: that is too much like accepting miracles *de re* . . . Eschewing vitalism and the magic touch of God's finger we rightly insist that it must be in virtue of some natural property of (organised) matter that parts of it get to be alive . . . It is a condition of adequacy on any account of the mind-body relation that it avoid assuming theism.[1]

Likewise, D. C. Dennett expresses distaste for

> . . . an asymmetrical scientific picture which includes, in one corner of the universe, basically *different*, non-physical entities which do not fall under the laws of physics.[2]

'Dualism,' Dennett says,

> the idea that minds (unlike brains) are composed of stuff that is exempt from the laws of physical nature, is a desperate vision which widely deserves its current disfavour.[3]

[119]

These basically *different* entities, lurking in corners of the universe where the laws of nature do not hold, are scary indeed.

Both McGinn and Dennett seem to assume that the only alternative to a physical explanation of any of the phenomena of human life is a supernatural one: if something cannot be explained by prior physical events in accordance with physical laws, the only way to explain it is in terms of causal action by God on a kind of stuff 'exempt' from the laws of nature.

We can see how this way of thinking arises. The word 'physical' comes from the Greek *phusikos* which we usually translate 'natural', and at least until the seventeenth century the words 'physical' and 'natural' could be used interchangeably. The discipline we call 'physics' Newton called 'natural philosophy'. If the physical is the same as the natural, any phenomenon or explanation which is non-physical is non-natural, and the step to calling it 'supernatural' seems uncontroversial. But since the seventeenth century the notions of the physical and the natural have moved apart. The physical contrasts on one side with the logical and the mathematical, on the other with the biological and the psychological – I use the term 'psychological' here to cover not only such functions as perception, self-awareness and intellectual thought but also purposive action and inaction. The natural too contrasts on one side with the logical and the mathematical, but on the other it contrasts with the supernatural; it includes the physical, but the biological and the psychological as well. Although in some contexts what is due to nature is set against what is due to human intervention, nobody seriously doubts that reasoning, generalising, fearing some outcomes and trying to bring about others, are all perfectly natural phenomena.

Physicalist philosophers feel that if these phenomena cannot be explained physically they cannot be natural at all. The supernatural comes right up to the physical, as savage jungle beasts might come up to our verandahs: there is no space between the physical and the supernatural for a natural sentient or intelligent life. Perhaps they would say that the supernatural does not really march with the physical because it does not exist at all: it is to be compared not to lions and tigers but to unicorns and chimaeras, whose threat to our verandahs is negligible. But why are they so sure that the supernatural does not exist? I think it is because they have a concept of it that is at best childish and at worst incoherent. Those who have seriously believed in the supernatural have also believed in a natural order that is non-physical, and their notion of the supernatural depends on this. I want to argue that their notion of the supernatural is coherent, and for that purpose it will be necessary to look at some of the objections to the idea that consciousness and purposive behaviour is natural but not physical.

To say that psychological phenomena belong to the physical domain is to say they can be explained physically. What does that entail? It is enough to say that their source is in our physical constituents, and they can be explained as the inevitable effect of action upon things constituted as we are by other things. This is not the way we normally explain each other's behaviour. We do that teleologically, in terms of reasons and purposes; that is, in terms of things the agent knows or believes to be the case and of objects of the agent's desires and aversions. We think that agents are conscious and purposive just insofar as their behaviour can be explained in these ways; and we think that acting for reasons and purposes is natural and not supernatural; teleological explanations are non-physical but not non-natural.

I shall now look at four considerations which lead philosophers to think that purposive behaviour must be explainable physically. Donald Davidson says:

> If I say that Smith set fire to the house in order to collect the insurance, I explain his action, in part, by giving one of its causes, namely his desire to collect the insurance.[4]

Davidson's reasoning, I think, is that 'Smith set fire to the house in order to collect the insurance' means the same as 'Smith set fire to the house because he wanted to collect the insurance', and the 'because' in this second sentence is understood as introducing a cause. Davidson would probably say also that in 'Smith set fire to the house because he knew it was insured for a fat sum', the 'because' introduces a cause. But that the 'because' does no such thing can be shown by a simple linguistic argument. In both these sentences, the main verb of the clause it introduces can be taken out of the clause and put in parentheses. We can say that Smith set fire to the house 'because, as he knew, it was insured for a fat sum' and 'in order that, as was his desire, he might collect the insurance'. We cannot do this in a sentence where the 'because' introduces a genuine cause. Davidson himself gives us an example: 'The house burnt down because Smith set fire to the bedding.' But how should we understand the sentences where 'because' does not introduce a cause? We should take the words 'because he wanted to' and 'because he believed that' as conjunctions like 'in order to' and 'for the reason that'.

Jonathan Bennett, David Papineau and others have proposed very ingenious analyses of sentences containing the teleological conjunctions 'in order that' and 'for the reason that' according to which use of these conjunctions really does imply that the behaviour explained is caused and explainable physically;[5] but they do not claim that we use the conjunctions in this way in our ordinary explanations of each other's behaviour. It would be absurd to claim this, since explanations in terms of reasons and purposes are offered by the most primitive people, people who have no idea of causal explanation at all, let alone the complicated kinds of causal explanation in terms of which these philosophers want to define being for a reason or purpose. What they are proposing is that, since physicalism is true, we should move over to these new conceptions. Whereas Davidson's analysis – or rather Spinoza's (*Ethics* 4, preface) – would, if defensible, be an argument for physicalism, theirs presupposes it.

Next, McGinn thinks that if purposive movements are not explainable physically, they must be miraculous, 'miracles *de re*'. This is not so much a reason for rejecting the possibility of something non-physical but natural as a simple ignoring of it. But I mention it because of the light it sheds on physicalist conceptions of the supernatural. A miracle, apparently, would be an event with a non-physical cause, and if anything happens because God so desires, God must cause it by non-physical action. In fact, the physical has to be defined in terms of the concepts we employ in causal understanding. The notions of a non-physical causal agent, non-physical causal action and non-physical causal conditions are all straightforwardly incoherent.

Dennett thinks that if any of our movements were not physically explainable we should have to be composed, at least in part, of stuff to which the laws of physics do not apply. To quote him again:

> If we proceed on the assumption that human and animal control systems are very complicated denizens of the physical universe, it follows that events within them . . . should be subject to explanation and prediction without recourse to meaning or intentionality.[6]

To be composed of physical stuff is indeed to be subject to physical laws, but it is not clear that for a thing to be subject to physical laws is for all its behaviour to be determined by action upon it in accordance with such laws. There are two kinds of physical law. First, those that deal with the fundamental physical forces of gravity, electricity and so on, tell us what causal action is necessary to prevent a certain outcome. If an object has a mass of two tons, then a pressure of two tons away from the centre of the earth is needed if it is not to approach the centre of the earth. Second, other physical laws tell us what certain causal action is sufficient to produce. If an object is composed of flesh and blood then (as Shylock says) cutting it is sufficient to produce bleeding, and putting it on the fire is sufficient to cause charring. But no physical law tells us that certain causal action is necessary to produce a given outcome.

The principle that every physical event is determined by another physical event in accordance with physical laws does imply that a given change will not occur unless there is some action sufficient to produce it. But this principle is not itself a physical law. Rather it aspires to being a metaphysical law, a principle that tells us something about physical laws, namely that nothing happens that cannot be explained in accordance with them. I know of no better attempt to prove this principle than that of Kant in *The Critique of Pure Reason*, which I find quite uncompelling. Someone who rejects it and thinks that some of our behaviour is not caused by action upon us, does not have to suppose that we are 'exempt' from physical laws of either of the kinds I have just distinguished. It is perfectly consistent to hold both that some of our behaviour is not caused by action on us, and that we are massive bodies composed of materials which are affected in various ways by various kinds of action.

But if that is so, must we not have in us some of Dennett's 'basically *different*' material? Tertullian, influenced perhaps by Stoicism, held that we are composed partly of soul-stuff, a non-physical kind of material, and this idea has been revived in our time by Richard Swinburne.[7] But the notion of stuff or material (*hulē*) is originally the notion of that out of which something arises, and subsequently the notion of that in a thing by virtue of which it changes independently of any purpose. The stuff out of which I arise or of which I am composed can play no part in explaining how my acting or refraining from action can be intentional, conscious or intelligent. Just as the concept of non-physical causation is self-contradictory so, I think, is the concept of non-physical material. Everything of which I am composed must be physical, since thinking of something as a component is thinking of it as having an explanatory role in a physical explanation.

The last reason I shall consider for denying there can be anything natural but non-physical may be gathered from Peter Carruthers. Here he is writing about scientists and purposive movements of our limbs:

> It is conceivable that when they trace the causal chain back up into events in the brain, there might come a point where the

[124]

causation just runs out into the sand, as it were. They might discover that a particular type of brain-event has no discoverable causal antecedents . . . We surely don't really expect that things will turn out like this. Do we not expect that the causal chain of bodily events caused by other bodily events will turn out to be unbroken? Are we not confident that every item in cellular activity will ultimately be causally explicable in terms of some prior physical stimulus?[8]

Carruthers does not tell us why we are so sure and confident about these things. To understand the feelings he expresses we must distinguish two kinds of physical explanation. Consider cases where an object changes from one state to another in a definite time, say two minutes. Sometimes we explain the change by causal action on the object throughout the time. The slice of bread changes colour from white to brown because the toaster acts on it thermally throughout the two minutes. Explaining a change by lack of contemporaneous action is similar. Suppose I engage in the terrifying joys of free-fall. I change from being near the aeroplane to being near the ground in two minutes because nothing is acting on me to keep me from the ground during those two minutes. That is one kind of explanation. But sometimes we explain a change as a continuation of a prior change. When one billiard ball hits a second, the movement of the second after the impact is a continuation of the movement of the first before, just as when a space rocket is moving uniformly its movement from the orbit of Jupiter to the orbit of Saturn is just a continuation of its movement from the orbit of Mars to that of Jupiter. Carruthers has in mind this second kind of explanation. What he is sure scientists will discover is that the movement of his hand when he writes is a continuation of electrical activity in his brain, which is a continuation of movements of impulses to his brain from his retina, which are continuations of movement of light particles to his retina from the sun and distant stars.

The principle that every process is a continuation of an earlier process is not a physical law but a special formulation of the metaphysical law that every change has a cause. It differs from the principle that every change is the result of simultaneous action (or absence of simultaneous action) on the thing changed. If we explain a change by simultaneous action we think that that action renders the change necessary or inevitable, whereas it would be irrational to think that an earlier stage of a process renders a later stage necessary. As both Aristotle and Hume insist, an earlier event cannot necessitate a later. The belief that it can is the confused belief that it is a natural law that the universe should continue to exist. When we explain a process as a continuation of an earlier process, instead of representing it as inevitable we are representing it as nothing new. The idea that there is nothing new under the sun fits a certain temperament or mood – it is powerfully expressed by the biblical writer Ecclesiastes (Eccles 1.1–11) – but it amounts less to understanding things than to reaching a viewpoint from which there is nothing to understand.

The more we think of understanding physically as seeing processes as mere continuations of earlier processes, the closer physical understanding will seem to mathematical. There is no physical necessity in mathematics. The Platonic dream that physical change might be explained in terms simply of mathematical properties – size, shape, distance, and velocity or extension in four dimensions – would involve explaining things as continuations. On the other an Aristotelian feeling for matter goes with trying to understand changes as the inevitable results of simultaneous action or inaction. Paradoxical as it may seem, the view of physical understanding that is the more materialistic is also the less jealous at the idea that there might be phenomena that are natural but not physically explainable. If we think that natural objects have in them a source of behaving in various ways when acted upon, and even when not acted upon, independently of any purpose, we will be readier to believe that some of them can act, independently of being acted upon, *for* purposes. I suspect that the modern philosophical mistrust of irreducibly teleological explanations springs as much from hostility to matter as from hostility to the supernatural;

it is just the latest manifestation of the traditional philosophical weakness for mathematics.

So much on the notion of the natural which, I claim, people had from the earliest times, before the physical was thought of, and still employ in their non-philosophical thinking today. I now pass to the supernatural. I have already made some negative points. A supernatural agent would not be one composed of non-physical material, and supernatural action would not be non-physical causation. These notions are incoherent, and if we look at the people who are generally agreed to believe in the supernatural we shall find they play hardly any role in their beliefs – indeed, these notions appear only when the believers are trying to think philosophically.

The paradigm supernaturalists, to whose beliefs we look when we wish to fix the meaning of the term 'supernatural', are the Jews and Christians. In their sacred writings the primary model for the supernatural is the cultivation and domestication of wild plants. The supernatural stands to the natural as the cultivated olive to the wild one; and God stands to intelligent, purposive nature as a planter of vines and pruner of fig trees stands to biological nature.

The first question a philosopher may ask here is: 'What is supernatural about this?' Education is supposed to turn savages into civilised beings and thoughtless, passionate children into intelligent, self-controlled adults; but education is natural, not supernatural. What is God, on the Judaeo-Christian view, except a patient, long-lived, but seldom actually seen headmaster?

To see in what way God is conceived as a supernatural person, we should start by looking at our notion of a natural person. By a 'person' here I mean an intelligent purposive agent. A natural person is a material object that is such an agent.

Two things make such persons natural. First, for anything for which I am morally responsible as a purposive agent, the material object that I am will be responsible as a causal agent. Any causal action which is for my purpose is action by some part of my body. Our limbs move as we desire, but nothing else does unless we move it using our limbs. Secondly, a natural person can act for a reason only if some part of that person's body is affected in a corresponding way. What do I mean by 'a corresponding way'? We move because of things we see and hear, and these are things that more or less directly affect our eyes and ears. We also move because of things we are told about or read about, so that words referring to them affect our eyes and ears. Sometimes a reason for acting can be almost complete illusory. I might put a horse-shoe over my door for the reason that there are demons in the neighbourhood that devour people whose doors are not protected by wrought iron or steel; and there might be no such demons anywhere. But I must have heard about these demons from people who affected my sense-organs.

Natural persons that are sentient have a further peculiarity. Some of their movements are for the purpose of producing or sustaining pleasant physical states of themselves, or terminating or avoiding unpleasant ones. Not all their purposive movements, however, are even indirectly for these purposes. Some are for the purpose of taking part in social life, and some for the purpose of benefiting other sentient or intelligent organisms. Though all the natural persons known to us are sentient, I do not see any impossibility in an intelligent agent that had the first two features but not this third: a material object to which no physical state of itself was an object of desire or aversion for its own sake. I should count such an agent as a natural person, though it could hardly be a organism generated by other organisms as we are.

A supernatural person would be an intelligent purposive agent lacking the constraints imposed by the first two features and presumably also lacking sentience as I have just described it. That is precisely how God is conceived by Christians and pretty consistently throughout the Old Testament. There is never any suggestion that God is sensitive to pleasant or unpleasant bodily sensations, whereas the so-called gods in Homer are highly sensitive to both: they experience pain when wounded by mortals or each other, and they revel in sex. The Judaeo-Christian God is an intelligent purposive agent. Almost everything that happens in the universe happens because he so desires, happens for his reasons and purposes. But he is not supposed to have any limbs with which he acts on anything – the action of the sun, the winds, etc., though he is morally responsible for it, is not action by parts of him – nor is he supposed to know what is the case in the universe by sense-perception. Having the three features of natural persons I described is what we believe it to be to have a body; the Judaeo-Christian God does not have a body.

Perhaps it will be said that God escapes being a natural purposive agent only through ceasing to be a purposive agent at all: the concept of a purposive agent without a body, or at least without the first two features of a natural person, is incoherent. Let me take these features in turn. First, could action be for the purposes of an agent if it was not the action of (or action caused by) a part of that agent's body? You can attribute action to me because it is the action of my hands; but if God has no limbs, how can we suppose that any action is the execution of his desires?

Hands are important for determining *who* is the person responsible for some purposive action, but not for determining whether it is purposive at all. If words appear on paper you think they were caused to appear on purpose because they are an English sentence; you understand their production as an exercise of knowledge how to write. If you see my hands produce them you attribute that knowledge to me. When we see graffiti we think the production of the words was purposive without attributing it to anyone. To be sure, though there may be no one in particular we think responsible, we think there were some hands at work. If we had good reason to think that no human hand had produced the words, we should come to doubt if they were made on purpose. But that is because we think, either that there are no supernatural persons, or that this particular writing on the wall is unworthy of such a person.

It is not really any harder to see how a supernatural agent can act purposively, than to see how a natural agent can. Consider the movement of my hand when I write. If we thought that to be purposive it must be caused by some further purposive action, we

[129]

should be in a vicious regress. What we judge purposive or mindless is the exercise of a causal power, a power to push or pull or heat. Our limbs push, pull and warm things with which they are in contact. Sometimes we think this action of theirs purposive, but whether it is purposive or not cannot depend on whether it is the exercise of a further causal power, the power to act causally on purpose. There could be no such causal power. There is such an ability as the ability to push a pen or heat food on purpose, but it is not a causal power; it is skill or technical knowledge, the art of the scribe or cook. What the theist attributes to God's desires is the exercise of causal powers by inanimate objects in accordance with physical laws, the heating of the sun, the downward pull of a suspended weight and so forth; and also the operations of the fundamental physical forces. If the sun heats and massive bodies approach for God's purposes, that is no more miraculous than if I approach my friend or my hands warm a brandy glass for my purposes, and no more requires an exercise of any further causal power.

No doubt action by my hand will be an exercise of my skill only if exercising it seems good to me. If you think my causing marks to appear on paper is purposive, you must think that the marks have a use – they form a meaningful sentence – and that I have a reason for using them. Now for this requirement to be met what is needed is knowledge or belief that something is the case, not muscle power or electricity; but this obliges us to consider the second feature of natural persons. They know what is the case by virtue of action on their sense-organs. If God has no sense-organs, how does he know what is the case in the universe? He is traditionally supposed to have the purpose of benefiting living organisms, or at least human beings: how does he know there are any? The traditional answer would be: because he put them there. God's knowledge of the universe may be conceived on the model of our knowledge of what we say or write. If I think I am saying something I can verify my belief by listening or playing back a tape, but the belief I am verifying is not derived from hearing. What I think I am saying is what I have decided to say or think it best to say. God would know that we are here because he thinks it best that physical processes should go on that result in complex organic structures like us.

Before I leave the conception of God as a supernatural person, a further point should be made. When we think that something is the work of a purposive agent we think it is an exercise of good or bad practical judgement and of greater or less skill and practical knowledge. We also think that natural agents acquire skill and judgment gradually, through practice. If natural processes generally go on because God wants them to, the natural order too must be an exercise of some kind of judgement and skill. Hume thought that a creator might have to acquire skill; in his lively way he suggests that the world might be 'only the first rude essay of some infant deity' (*Dialogues* 5). But acquiring basic skills is learning how to use an existing natural order, and natural prudence is a matter of discerning what is best for existing organisms. The production of a complete natural order and the conception of a system of living organisms could not be an exercise of acquired prudence or folly, acquired skill or systematic inefficiency; it would have to be the work of a supernatural kind of wisdom or folly. This supernatural wisdom would not be fully comprehensible by human beings, a point made frequently in the Old Testament, and most eloquently in the Book of Job; but we think it rather wisdom than folly if the physical universe and the organisms in it seem to us admirable rather than contemptible – and conversely if we are not impressed by that natural world we are not likely to ascribe it to a supernatural source.

In Judaeo-Christian thinking God is a supernatural agent and acts with supernatural wisdom. But the supernatural does not stop there. God raises our life to a supernatural level. At first it may seem that this claim involves a different conception of the supernatural. We saw that it is explained by analogy with the difference between wild and cultivated life, and that seems quite unrelated to the difference between having and not having a body. If, indeed, God enables us to live on after death, there *will* be a link, since a post-mortem existence, even with a resurrected body, will hardly

[131]

be body-dependent like the existence of a natural person. But God is supposed to make our lives supernatural even before death, and an examination of the coherence of ascribing a supernatural existence to human beings should start with life in the natural world.

There is nothing supernatural about acting out of duty, taking part in social life, or acting altruistically: that is the wild fruit on which the divine gardener works. The Old Testament attaches value to caring for the poor and weak, gentleness, humility and a will to change one's way of life for the better, but these are natural virtues. Whereas, however the domestication of wild plants does not call for any efforts by the plants, the raising of human nature to a higher level requires human beings to want to change, and use their natural powers to cooperate with God. The emphasis on care for the poor and humility reflects the idea that we cooperate by concentrating on altruistic behaviour, not success and status in human societies. How, then, does human life become supernatural?

This question is ambiguous. We could be asking, 'What can be supernatural about human life? What can justify calling it "supernatural"?' Or, 'By what action on human beings does the divine gardener make their lives supernatural?' Let me start with the first question.

The Old Testament Jews believed they had a covenant with God that made them into a supernatural society. Exodus 19.3 describes them as a holy nation, a kingdom of priests. Under the covenant they have duties to God, to keep the Ten Commandments and the rest of the divine law, and God has duties to them, to guide them, give them rules of conduct, and protect them (Lev 26.3–13). They interpret their history in the light of this. Calamities are the consequence of disobedience, periods of prosperity the result of repentance and divine compassion. In the preface to his *Antiquities of the Jews*, Josephus says his work will show that 'actions piously designed will turn out prosperously', whereas those who deviate from God's commands 'will be frustrated in their designs and expectations'. This pious declaration is not a commonplace of ancient historians: we do not find it in Polybius, whom Josephus

[132]

admired – Polybius puts emphasis on Fortune (*Tuche*) rather than divine justice (*History*, 1.4, etc.) – or in Thucydides or Tacitus. And while Homer speaks of human rulers as 'shepherds of the people' the Homeric gods do not play that social role; at most they have friendly concern for individuals.

But in what way, precisely, is the social life of the Old Testament Jews supernatural? In the first place, God's action in guiding and protecting them is presumably supernatural. But this action is owed to them under the covenant; it is part of the life of the society. So their own action in keeping the divine law is sharing in a communal life that is at least partly supernatural. It is supernatural by association. And not by association only: it differs in intrinsic character from keeping human laws. The commandments to offer sacrifices to God and keep the Sabbath clearly require them to think of God as their ruler and liberator; and the commandments to honour parents and refrain from homicide, theft, adultery, etc., require them to think of each other not just as fellow members of a human family or nation but as God's creatures and members of his chosen race. The life is supernatural partly because it is the life of a collectivity with a supernatural member, and partly because a supernatural agent comes into the description of its goals.

The New Testament also envisages a supernatural society, a 'kingdom of heaven' under a new covenant with God, but there is a further idea in the New Testament which is not present, or at least not prominent, in the Old: members of this society share in God's life and live with it. This participation in God's life is mediated by Christ, but none the less real for that. According to John, Christ prays that his followers 'may be in us as you, Father, are in me and I in you' that they 'may be one as we are one, with me in them and you in me' (Jn 17.21–3; cf. 26). Similarly, Paul says in Galatians, 'It is not I that live, but Christ lives in me.' (Gal 2.20; see also Rom 8.9–11, 1 Cor 12.27, Eph 2.5–6.)

How are we to conceive this sharing in God's life? John's Gospel offers the model of a vine (Jn 15.1–6); the branches of the vine are in the vine and share its life. This, perhaps, can illustrate only the way in which members of a society share in the life of the society. But Christ also says, in rather mysterious language that is usually taken to allude to the Eucharist:

> If you do not eat the flesh of the son of man and drink his blood, you will not have life in yourselves. The person who chews my flesh and drinks my blood has eternal life, and I will raise him up on the last day. My flesh is true food and my blood is true drink. The person who chews my flesh and drinks my blood remains in me and I in him. As the Father sent me, so I live through the Father, and the person who chews me, he too will live through me. (Jn 6.53–7)

The union these words describe does not sound like the unity of a society. A better model than the vine is that of the bridegroom or lover, also imported into the New Testament from the Old. The lover cares for the beloved as an individual, and makes her flowering his goal; Christ seems to describe a similar identification with the individual Christian.

What can this mean in practice? Since God is supposed to be responsible for the natural order generally, sharing in his life ought to be sharing this responsibility. If natural processes go on because God wants them to, for the benefit of living organisms, we should share in his life if they went on partly because we want them to, and for the benefit of organisms for which we are concerned. But it is supposed to be because God so desires, not only that natural processes generally go on, but also that there are living organisms, and not only that there are living organisms, but that human beings rise from a natural to a supernatural level. If we can share responsibility for this, that will be sharing in a special way in God's life. Now Christians clearly believe that they can share responsibility at least to a certain extent for each other's moral and spiritual development, since this is the object of many of their prayers. They pray that other people will recognise what is true and do what is right. And they believe even more obviously that they can share responsibility for their own progress from the natural to the supernatural

[134]

since they think (or most of them think) that unless they cooperate and are willing to accept God's gifts he can do nothing with them. The activity of uniting themselves to God is itself already supernatural.

The suggestion that human beings might share in God's creative and sanctifying activity, and that this might be what justifies calling their life 'supernatural', may sound like a delusion of grandeur. Certainly it seems to give urgency to the second question I distinguished: 'By what action on human beings can their life be made supernatural?' That question, as we understand it today, could hardly have occurred to the Jews either of the Old or of the New Testament, since it depends on a notion of causal explanation which is lacking in the Bible. It is similar to the questions 'What do we *do* in order to think? *By what action of what upon what* do we believe things or desire things?' Just as these latter questions involve a misunderstanding of thought, so 'By doing what to us does God raise our lives to a supernatural level?' involves a misunderstanding of the Judaeo-Christian conception of the supernatural. Supernatural life is supposed to be a supernatural development or enhancement of natural. Natural life's coming to be supernatural must be conceived on the model of purposeless activity's coming to be purposive. If there can be no process by which action is made to be purposive, there can be no process by which action for natural purposes is transformed into action for supernatural purposes. When Christians became acquainted with concepts of causal explanation and natural law, to explain how our natures are transformed they did not appeal to the notion of a miracle or intervention in the physical order; they excogitated a theory of 'grace', *charis* or *gratia*. As the abilities to perceive natural things and to desire or be averse to natural events are natural endowments, so the intellectual ability to see ourselves, other people and the physical world generally in relation to God, and the love of God we need in order to act according to this vision, were classed, under the names 'faith' and 'charity', as supernatural gifts.

The theology of grace is an ethereal region into which a philosopher's wings can hardly carry him. But whereas the first Christians did not ask by what action on them God might make them into supernatural agents, they did ask by what action on their own part they might become such agents, and to that the answer was simple and down to earth. They could share in God's life by acts of cult, *threskeia*, and also by living according to the Christian moral code. They must cherish the people in their families and perform so called corporal and spiritual works of mercy, such as sheltering the homeless and counselling people in uncertainty. These things can be done merely out of concern for the human beneficiaries. In that case the agent acquires merely a natural responsibility for the beneficiary's life. But the agent can have the additional purpose of doing what God wants and being united with God after death. If there is no God, that is acting under an illusion; but if there is a God and Christians are right about his purposes, perhaps they really do become responsible for their beneficiaries' lives supernaturally as well; their works become prayers.

Life before death is clearly possible, but philosophers have difficulty in seeing how it can be supernatural. Life after death would be supernatural, sure enough, but philosophers question whether it is possible. Part of their difficulty, however, comes from conceiving it almost exactly as we tend to conceive natural life in the distant future, something at which we are not at all good.

We can easily imagine how things will be in ten or twenty years' time. Hardly anyone can imagine clearly a world three hundred years hence and as different from ours as ours is from that of the English Civil War. When it comes to imagining a world a thousand years hence, or twenty thousand, or two million, I defy anyone to tell the difference. There are perhaps four thousand million people on the earth at the moment. We probably expect about the same number twenty thousand years from now. But with luck they will be healthier than we are and live longer. So it will be an elderly population with few children. Somehow it seems unlikely that in twenty thousand years' time anyone will be living in pleasant old country houses like those now inhabited in England, beside the

Dordogne or among the Tuscan hills. More probably, people will be living in blocks of flats, or in hotels with bathrooms *en suite* above sunny beaches. What will they do? Not much work, because everything will be so automated. They will swim in the pool, play games, have sex, and watch an improved kind of television; and they will go on doing these things for hundreds and hundreds of years. What difference do philosophers suppose there to be between this vision of the future, and the vision religious people have of life after death? Only, perhaps, that in heaven people do not have sex, but see God instead.

It is extremely difficult to believe that the distant future will really be as I have described. It seems more likely that the human race will destroy itself utterly, or regress to the primitive condition of chimpanzees, than that it will perpetuate itself for millions of years like this. How much harder it is to believe in an existence like this for the dead. Think of the size of the hotels there would have to be in heaven a million years hence if at any moment between then and now there are four thousand million people waiting to die! Think of the vapidity of the interminable lives! As for seeing God, is it on television in their rooms, or at a mammoth press-conference of billions of souls, or by taking turns in one-to-one interviews? There would be long waits for those.

In Judaeo-Christian thought, life after death is life in union with God. This union should not be conceived on the model of spatial proximity; it should be sharing more fully in God's life than is possible for human beings before death. If the dead live with God's life it should not be a problem how, without sense-organs, they can have knowledge of the world and other people: they will share God's knowledge of these things. Christians who believe that God knows what they are doing and thinking, and that their dead friends are united with God either as unsevered branches are united with the vine or in an even closer way, can hardly avoid the conclusion that their dead friends know what they are doing and thinking. God's knowledge is practical; he is not a detached observer. So union with him would require the dead to participate

[137]

in his activity as well as his knowledge. What has been said about supernatural life before death can be extended to life after it.

T. Penelhum argued that there would be nothing to differentiate one bodiless person from another.[9] One ground for saying that is that physical bodies or chunks of space-time are the only things different of themselves, and everything else must be differentiated by means of them. That seems to be false; certainly it is difficult to believe that chunks of space really exist independently of bodies. But if all dead people had exactly the same purposes as each other and as God, there might be no reason for thinking that something happened because one person wanted it rather than because another; no means of differentiating the activities of different supernatural agents. In fact, however, each person before death acquires a different set of concerns, and could be assigned a share in what happens corresponding to that.

A way of conceiving this is provided by the theory of monads, as proposed by Leibniz.[10] A modern reader of Leibniz might explain it like this. First, imagine a story, say Shakespeare's *Henry V*, filmed simultaneously from the standpoint of each of the actors, Henry, Pistol, Katherine and the thirty or so other people who have parts. We can imagine a camera fixed between each person's eyes, so that it films just what that character could see. Now, suppose thirty or forty viewers, each in a room by himself, with no light and nothing but a television screen. (They would be rooms in Hilbert's Hotel if the theory is to be modelled in detail.) Each viewer sees on his screen the film shot from the point of view of one of the characters. Although the viewers would in fact be in spatial relations – I might be in room 5 and you just opposite in room 6 – the spatial relations between the viewers would have nothing at all to do with the spatial relations of the things they see. Perhaps I see the things the hostess, Mistress Quickly, sees, and you see the things that Alice, Katherine's maid, sees, and they are never anywhere near each other. Leibniz wanted his monads to be like the viewers except that in themselves they are not spatially related at all; they each see mental pictures of the same sequence of events

[138]

from different points of view. Applying this to our own problem we may say that in their natural lives people have friends and relatives, they visit different countries, they learn about societies other than their own and take an interest in people removed from them in time or place. These things come to stand to them not only in spatio-temporal relations but in relations of practical importance; they owe more to some people than others or care more about them. As what you and I see when viewing *Henry V* in our hotel bedrooms depends on the position in the spatio-temporal order of the characters from whose viewpoint we are seeing events, the positions of Mistress Quickly and Alice, so what the dead are responsible for could depend on the order of priorities they established before death.

To illustrate this, suppose that my mother died and was united with God before I married. If my marrying and having children were known to God, these things would be known to her, and she would have concern for my wife and children. They would be known to her through God but also through me. My wife's ancestors might have the same concern for my children, but their knowledge and concern would run through my wife. Not that they would be unaware of me; but they would know me too through my wife, and through me in turn they could be aware of my dead forebears and share their concern for me. Similarly, if my wife and I take delight in the same natural phenomenon, say the same sunset, her dead friends could share in the enjoyment of the sunset through her and mine through me; and we might owe the spectacle to them as well as to God.

It is a widespread religious belief that the dead take an interest in what happens in the natural world: people pray to their ancestors or to the saints, the dead that are 'with God', for help. They do not think that life after death consists solely in acting in the natural world with God, or that all thought is targeted ultimately on natural things. I have not said anything about beliefs and desires that remain within the supernatural sphere (or about the supernatural bodies Christians postulate on the strength of the Gospel accounts of the risen Christ). But speculation about the details of life after death is speculative indeed. What is important for my present purposes is whether the notion of it is coherent at all. Could a human being participate to any extent in God's life without being a causal agent with a body, and without loss of identity in God? Having a body does not explain how we can act in a natural way for reasons and purposes, though it is part of acting naturally to have a body. Still less does it explain how we can act in a supernatural way. The fundamental idea expressed in the images of the divine gardener, shepherd and lover is that while we are alive and act causally we can participate in supernatural life up to a point: we have purposes that do not depend on our being causal agents, and our limbs move for these purposes. If that idea is coherent, I do not see why changes should not take place for our purposes without our being causal agents at all.

EIGHT

The Trinity and the Tripartite Soul

According to the Second Council of Constantinople (2 June 553) there is 'one divinity in three hypostases or persons'. Today, it is commoner to say that there are three persons in one God. No doubt these formulations come to the same thing, but what is that?

The English word 'person' translates the Latin *persona* and the Greek *prosopon*, expressions for the masks actors wore on the ancient stage. Since the same actor might appear in different masks, playing different roles, in the same play, the word suggests that the Persons of the Trinity, the Father, Son and Spirit, are three roles the one God plays, three appearances or aspects he presents. The word 'hypostasis' is a philosophical term for something that exists on its own like a living organism; so to call the Father, Son and Spirit 'hypostases' is to suggest that they form a kind of three-membered society. Both these suggestions are unorthodox. The first is Sabellianism, the second tritheism, and these are the Charybdis and Scylla between which the speculative theologian is supposed to steer. But is such a course possible? The use of both terms by Constantinople II rather poses the problem than solves it.

Do we need to solve it? In these days when speculative theologians look more to Heidegger and Wittgenstein than to Augustine or Aquinas, attempts to capture Christian beliefs in propositional

[141]

formulations arouse misgivings. Should we even try to state a consistent doctrine of the Trinity? If what I shall be arguing is correct, Christians cannot afford not to make the attempt. They are committed by a tradition of belief and practice which goes back to pre-Christian Judaism to three distinct conceptions of God, and if these cannot be reconciled in a doctrine of the Trinity, the whole of their religious thinking lies open to charges of confusion and incoherence.

What is true is that religious beliefs should not be conceived on the model of theoretical beliefs about mathematics or physics. The belief that there are three Persons in God is not like the belief that there are three quarks in the proton, or three prime numbers between 2 and 10. A theist is one who holds that the universe depends on a divine person, a person not in the ancient sense of a mask, but in the modern sense of an intelligent, purposive agent. Theology may be a theoretical discipline, but actual beliefs about God are like our beliefs about the people and animals around us. Such beliefs are all practical in character: they all involve interpersonal engagement, sympathy or antipathy.

That is recognised up to a point in the first great attempt to give a philosophical account of the doctrine of the Trinity. Augustine looks for models for the divine Persons in the human psyche. He moves from a lover, the beloved and love, through a mind that knows and loves itself to a division of mind into memory, understanding and will. But he does not consider the practical aspect of attributing mind to human beings – he does not seem to see any radical difference between thinking someone an intelligent, purposive agent and thinking something round or square – and though anyone who reads the *De Trinitate* must be impressed by Augustine's intellectual honesty and perseverance, I think few will feel he deals adequately with the ontological status of the one God and the three Persons. Lovers and knowers are persons in the modern sense, whereas memory, understanding and love are capacities, dispositions or activities.

Augustine is not the only trisector of the human psyche. A different division was proposed by Plato in the *Republic* and arrived at much later and more or less independently by Freud. In my opinion the Plato-Freud trisection (at least if properly developed) is extremely useful for the purpose for which it was originally designed, namely to obtain insight into purposive human behaviour with a view to improving it. I shall argue here that it can also be used to shed light on the doctrine of the Trinity. And I shall not overlook the practical dimension. I shall try to show how our practical thinking about other human beings requires us to distinguish three psychic 'parts', and then suggest that traditional beliefs about God require Christians to distinguish, not three divine parts, but three divine Persons.

Plato divides the psyche into a Desiring Part, a Spirited Part (the *thumoeides*) and a Reasoning Part; these correspond roughly to Freud's Id, Superego and Ego respectively. I have argued elsewhere[1] that the best way of understanding this is as a division between types of motivation or ways in which we can be motivated. Sometimes we act (or refrain from acting) in order to obtain something that benefits us or to avoid something bad for us as more or less isolated individuals. Painful sensations are objects of aversion to us and pleasant sensations objects of desire, independently of any consequences, and the unimpeded exercise of intelligence and skill is another kind of pleasure we seek for its own sake as solitary individuals. A second kind of motivation is duty. When we have a duty to do something, doing it becomes an end in itself, and when we have a duty to refrain from doing something doing it becomes an object of aversion for its own sake. Whereas we seek pleasure and shun pain and boredom as solitary egoists, duty motivates us as social beings (and conversely we live as social beings in living with an eye to the rules and customs of our society). Thirdly, we sometimes act as altruists out of disinterested concern for other intelligent or sentient beings (and in exceptional cases we can act out of disinterested malice). That others should achieve what is good for them, whether as egoists, as social beings or as altruists, becomes an end in itself to us: their goals become ours.

[143]

This differentiation of ways in which we are motivated does not, strictly speaking, entail a division of the human agent into parts. We do not think that one part of us pursues what is good for the individual and another does what is a duty; rather, a single human agent sometimes acts egoistically and sometimes dutifully, and much human behaviour is a compromise between egoistic, dutiful and altruistic motivations. So it might be feared that using this trisection as a model for the Trinity will inevitably lead to a Sabellian doctrine. Certainly, it will involve steering closer to that hazard; whether we must be caught by it remains to be seen.

The account I have sketched is highly theoretical: how in practice do we think of people as egoists, social beings and altruists? In all three cases we ourselves think as altruists. I cannot think that a cat, or even an insect, is moving to avoid pain without either feeling concern and wanting it to escape the pain, or feeling cruel joy and wanting it to suffer. That is part of what it is to think that something is *for the sake of* something: such teleological understanding is incompatible with indifference. And if thinking of others as acting egoistically involves disinterested concern, so, *a fortiori*, does thinking of them as acting out of duty or altruism. It is part of our normal intelligent understanding of the behaviour of our friends in practical perplexity to ascribe motivations to them of all three kinds. Perhaps only a philosopher can state lucidly how they differ, but we all learn how to balance them against one another.

The way in which I wish to apply the psychological distinction to God is simple. I would compare the Father to a human being acting as an egoist, the Son to one acting as a social being, and the Spirit to one acting disinterestedly to benefit others. I shall first show how these comparisons illuminate what is traditionally said and thought about the divine Persons, and then try to clear my account of the charge of Sabellianism.

There is a folk song which contains the words 'One is one and all alone and ever more shall be so.' I do not know if the words are intended to refer to God, but they express a conception of God we sometimes find in the Old Testament. He has no origin himself and is the origin of everything else, acting alone. Later thinkers conceive of God as having a life independent of creation. When they ask themselves in what this life consists, they tend to model it on theoretical human thinking, like pure mathematics. If God is above considering the properties of numbers and shapes, perhaps he thinks about his own nature as an intelligent being. Now, it would, of course, be impossible for us to do mathematics if we did not live in societies and have friends. Still, theoretical thinking is something we enjoy as fairly solitary individuals and so is artistic creation. So insofar as we think of God as a creator and a contemplative thinker, we think of him as a sort of egoist.

How far, and in what practical context, do we think of God in this way? To think he created the universe is not to think he made it out of pre-existent material, still less out of a non-material called 'nothing'; it is not to have a cosmological hypothesis. It is to think that natural processes begin and go on because he so desires; that he is responsible for them as we are for the limb movements we make on purpose. For what purposes do we think he wants the course of nature to continue? Perhaps he finds creation enjoyable as we can find it enjoyable to write or to read what we have written. But surely he chiefly has in view the good of the organisms that arise in the course of nature.

Now, if I think that your hands are moving in order that there may be an interesting novel I must think either that the words which appear on the page constitute such a novel, in which case I might say 'That's good. Go on!'; or I must think your are writing trash, and try to dissuade you. Psalms like 93, 104 and 148 show a reaction like the first to the divine creation. They do not encourage God to proceed – that would be patronising – but they are exclamations of admiration.

If I think you are breeding birds, say, for the benefit of the birds, either I think the project worthwhile, want it to succeed and care for the birds, or I think it a waste of time and detest the birds. If we think God wants the course of nature to continue for the benefit of living organisms we no longer think of him purely as an egoist: we attribute altruism to him, and perhaps we cannot attribute to him a creative part without also attributing to him an altruistic. But in any case, the belief that creation is for the benefit of living creatures involves either concern for creatures generally or hostility to them. In the psalms I have mentioned, and in many other places in the Old Testament like God's speech in Job and the hymn of the young man in the blazing furnace, we find an exultant enthusiasm for even those living organisms least useful or most dangerous to human beings, and a desire to give life even to inanimate nature — 'Look at Behemoth, what strength he has in his loins, what power in his stomach muscles' (Job 40.15–16); 'Praise God from the earth, sea monsters and all the depths, fire and hail, snow and mist, storm winds that obey his word' (Ps 148.7–8; cf. Dan 3.52ff) — these are utterances that express the belief that God created heaven and earth.

But there are other Old Testament prayers that reveal a completely different conception of God. He appears as a person who has entered into verbal communication with human beings, especially with Abraham and his descendants, and who has made covenants with the Jewish nation. Under these covenants the Jews are bound to keep certain rules and offer certain sacrifices; while God for his part is bound to protect them and support them against other nations and their tutelary powers (Lev 26.3–13; Deut 28.1–14). God is the god of the Jews, they are his people, and in this context he is frequently angry with them and asked to have pity on them. Although the two conceptions of the universal creator and the tribal protector are often blended, as in Psalms 33, 89 and 147, the difference between them to the modern reader is patent. Many people feel that while the notion of an unapproachable creator is edifying and sublime, the notion of the tribal god who experiences anger, jealousy and pity is primitive and disreputable.

What is less noticeable is that the notion of duty has no place in thinking of God as the universal creator. A creator has no duties to creatures. A creator can be kind or cruel, but kindness and cruelty motivate us as altruists; being kind and refraining from cruelty is not a duty but a kind of rationality. Neither have creatures as such any duties towards their creator. Duties are attached by societies to various relationships and roles, and different societies attach different duties to the same role or relationship – to wives, say, or doctors, or old women or lunatics. The relationship of creator to creature is not one in which two members of a society can stand to one another; neither is being a creator a social role.

Perhaps it will be felt that creatures have duties to their creator in gratitude. But what is gratitude? Either it is returning such benefits as is customary or obligatory in society; or it is the particular friendly concern one feels for an agent who has benefited one in the past, such as the lion felt for Androcles. The lion had no duty to Androcles but only goodwill arising out of Androcles's former kindness to it. In some societies people have a duty to worship the gods, but that is a duty they owe to other members of their society, not to the gods themselves, and to Aristotle, at least, the notion of friendly concern for gods seemed ridiculous. As soon as we start thinking we owe anything to God we have moved from the notion of God as universal creator to a much more anthropomorphic conception.

No conception could be more anthropomorphic than the Christian conception of Christ. But it may be thought that the human form of the incarnate Son is entirely a consequence of his incarnation during the reign of Augustus. That was not quite the opinion of the early Fathers. They thought they descried the Son intervening in human affairs in the Old Testament. According to Eusebius (*Ecclesiastical History* 1.2.7–13) it is he who appears to Abraham at Genesis 18.1, wrestles with Jacob at Genesis 32.26 and addresses Moses from the burning bush at Exodus 3.1–6; similarly, Irenaeus (*Contra Haereses* 4.10.1). These speculations have not become orthodoxy; but it is significant that when Old Testament writers wish to show God addressing human beings in words they like him to do so not directly but through a 'messenger' who seems not to be a creature, as angels are conventionally conceived to be, but divine (Gen 16.7, 22.11; Ex 14.19; Num 22.22; Judg 2.1; Wis 18.15.

Christians certainly believe they have duties to Christ as head of the society he founded; they are bound by his commandments as their lord and teacher. But do they have duties only to the Son and not to the Father? Not exactly. Christ as priest of the society he founded has the duty of offering worship to the Father, and other human beings have a duty to offer it through and with him.

The problem that faces those who believe that the universe depends on a personal creator is that there can be communication with people and obligation to them only when there is society with them, and creatures can have no society with their creator. The Christian solution to this problem is surprising. It depends on a duplication of divine Persons. The God who enters into communication and social relations with us and to whom we owe obedience is not the God who is worshipped but an intermediary who worships. The creator can be worshipped because he has a relationship to this intermediary, and because the intermediary also has relations with creatures they can worship through him. They acquire an adoptive relationship to the creator.

Christ regularly uses a word meaning 'father' to refer to God. He means it to refer, not to one member of the Trinity, something of which his hearers knew nothing, but simply to the one God of Jewish monotheism. Part of his purpose in using it, however, is to claim a relationship to the creator analogous to the father-son relationship recognised in all or nearly all human societies. That has a biological basis in begetting, and theologians looking for a model for the relationship between the divine Persons try to find something comparable with begetting. It is traditional to propose a thinker's formation or production of a concept. Elsewhere[2] I have suggested a modification of this: a conscious agent's decision to be a person of a particular sort. We say that the child is father to the man, meaning that I am responsible when young for the adult personality I acquire, for the purposive agent I come to be. We can compare a human being's decision to be a person of a certain sort, a person who will act because of certain sorts of reason and in spite of others, to God's decision to be a God that has society with creatures. The God who speaks to them and instructs them is the offspring of that decision; and he can be faithful to himself as decider and accept the duties of an intermediary.

We must think of God as a social being if we want to communicate with him and worship him, even if as a social being he is rather the intermediary than the ultimate addressee of our prayers. And there is another way in which Christians must think of God as a social being. They aspire to a supernatural life with him that can continue after death. Some Christians have no doubt imagined this on the model of life in a pleasant suburb. In heaven we shall each have our own detached villa to which we can withdraw and from which, when we feel sociable, we can emerge to visit God or our dead friends and relatives. But there is a tradition that to transcend our mortal condition we must actually share in God's life. A model for this is not a suburb but a living organism – Christ uses a vine as an example (John 15.1–5, which looks back, of course, to many passages in the Old Testament prophets). A branch of the vine shares in the life of the whole, but does so only by being united with the other branches and the trunk.

Life which is shared in this way, which we have as parts of a larger living thing, is social life. I share in the life of a human society when doing what that society holds to be my duty appears to me good as an end in itself, and doing what it prohibits appears shameful or horrible. Christ announces the inauguration of a supernatural society (the 'kingdom of heaven') which like human societies has rules and customs. We would share in its life by living with regard to its rules. But in addition Christ instituted sacraments, above all the Eucharist, by receiving which Christians are supposed to share in his divine life. In passages like John 6 Christ teaches that it is only through union with himself that we can participate in the life of God. Keeping his rules and receiving the sacraments we have the same life as he, so if he is God as a social being we have the same life as God. But, at least on the face of it, there is no other way in which we could share directly in the life of the creator. Our notion of a sharable life comes from biological organisms, and that sort of life cannot be attributed to God as creator at all, but it must be to any person that acts as a social being.

To suggest that the second Person of the Trinity is God as a social being is not, of course, to imply that if Christ was an incarnation of that person he can have acted only as a social being. As a man he must have had an egoist and an altruist part to his psyche, and the Gospels plainly show him as sensitive to hunger, thirst and pain and as acting out of concern for individuals, for instance at Cana and Bethany. Nevertheless it is significant that they represent him as a model for us chiefly as social beings. He loves his nation and its capital city without chauvinism; he is conscientious in performing his religious duties but is neither bigoted nor uncritical of customary practices. We are not told that he had striking qualities as an individual, that he was strong, good looking or particularly skilful either at intellectual or at manual tasks. But he has outstanding courage and loyalty, virtues which attach to us principally as social beings, and he is conspicuously free from the vices that attack us in that capacity, greed for power and status, snobbery, cowardice and fear of public opinion.

The conception of a universal creator is different from that of an anthropomorphic tribal god, but so is a third notion of God found in the Bible.

> You overlook people's sins, so that they can repent. You love everything that exists, and nothing that you have made disgusts you (Wis 11.24–6).

Besides speaking of God as his personal father, Christ describes him as a loving and compassionate parent, endlessly forgiving, who cares for all living creatures as individuals (for example, Mt 6.12 and 10.29–31). People often feel that there is an irresoluble tension between these passages and those which speak of God as imposing on people rules that admit of no exceptions and inflicting

[150]

punishment on them for breaking these rules. They may also feel that a creator would not be an angry, punitive judge, but that is less because he would have concern for every organism as an individual than because he would have no concern for creatures at all. The nature of a creator would be like that of the Epicurean gods:

> *Ipsa suis pollens opibus, nil indiga nostri,*
> *Nec bene promeritis capitur nec tangitur ira.*[3]

Christ's use of the word 'father' may make a modern reader connect God's concern for individuals chiefly with the Person of the Father. But, as I have said, Christ did not assume in his hearers a knowledge of a plurality of divine Persons; at most he wants them to see that a notion like that of parental concern for the individual child applies to the one God. This conception of God is most powerfully expressed, both in the Old Testament and in the New, through the image of God's breath.

'You take back your breath and they die and revert to dust; you send out your breath and life begins.' (Ps 104.29–30.) Breath here symbolises or actually carries life, and the idea is that God gives life to creatures by putting his own life into them.[4] This is different both from creation, in which physical processes go on because that is God's desire, and from entering into society with creatures. In the Pauline epistles the divine breath of life becomes the Spirit that dwells in the faithful (Rom 8.9) and is the source, not just of our natural vital functions and artistic creativity (cf. Ex 31.3), but of knowledge of God (1 Cor 2.10–16), of non-egoist behaviour (Gal 5.17–24), and in general of divine life. (Rom 8.12; 8.14–15; Gal 4.6–7.)

These passages do not describe sharing in a common life, however supernatural. The point is not that we all live in a larger whole but that God lives in each of us. To believe this we must conceive God as acting as we do when we act altruistically. It is significant that in Romans 5.5 the Spirit is given us by God out of *agape*, the Pauline term for disinterested concern. When we act out of concern for others we identify ourselves with them as agents, that is, their achieving their goals becomes our goal. But we cannot actually act within other agents. We can only help them, removing obstacles or evils or giving them information or pleasure. But the Christian belief about God's gift of the Spirit is that God can work for our well-being from within us.

The wording of the letter in Acts 15 indicates the different ways in which the first Christians thought of the Son and the Spirit:

> We have decided unanimously to elect delegates and send them to you with our well beloved Barnabas and Paul, who have committed their lives to the name of our Lord Jesus Christ . . . It has been decided by the Holy Spirit and by ourselves not to impose on you any burden beyond these essentials . . . (Acts 15.25–8).

The name of their Lord Jesus is that of a leader they follow and obey; the Spirit is not a person they obey but is present in them as officers of Christ and members of a deliberative body: their decisions are the Spirit's.

The Psalmist's picture of God animating creatures by filling them with his own breath may seem unsatisfying to the modern Christian in two ways. First, we do not think God has breath: the model we are offered for his action in the individual is physical, and when we remove physical interaction from it nothing is left. Second, if God did breathe life into us as we breathe air into a balloon, it would be his life, not ours, as it is our breath in the balloon, not the balloon's. But the belief that God acts in us out of concern for us must be taken along with the belief that we share in the life of God as a social being. Even at the natural level social and altruistic motivations complement each other. Acts of kindness create social duties and social relationships foster individual friendships. The rules of society help us to resist egoist emotions when they move us to act cruelly or disrespectfully, and concern for individuals helps us to resist the social motives of ambition, competitiveness and fear of disapproval, and to break or try to change such rules as there is reason to change. In Christian belief the relation between sharing in a social life with Christ and having God act in us is simple and intimate. By keeping Christ's commandments and receiving the sacraments we welcome the Spirit into us, and the more the Spirit dwells in us the easier it is to live according to the Christian code.

Christianity supplements the model of artificial respiration, in which the person being revived is passive, with the model of a bridal couple. Bride and groom are in fact united, or should be, both as social beings, since in every society the marriage relationship carries duties, and as altruists, since they are supposed to care for each other as individuals. Christ refers to himself as a bridegroom (Mt 19.15, etc.) and seems to have in mind primarily the social aspect. He seems to think of himself as the bridegroom of the people of God, as is the tribal god of the Jews in some Old Testament texts (Is 54.5–6; Hos 2.4; etc.). But bride and groom receive each other sexually, and this reception can be the expression of their concern for each other as individuals. In particular each desires to experience pleasant sensations, and desires this not just as an egoist, but because it is what the other desires. That the beloved should experience pleasure is an end in itself to the lover, and therefore doubly an end in itself to the beloved who reciprocates loving concern. In the same way the creature can desire to receive the gifts of God and what theologians call 'grace', not just because they are beneficial, but to fulfil God's desire to benefit.

It is possible, of course, to want to share in the life of the Christian community out of concern for Christ, because that is what he wanted for us. But it seems that he chiefly wanted us to share in the life of the community because through that we have the Spirit present in us as individuals. The remarks reported at John 16, which follow his use of the image of the vine, strongly suggest that he desires the plenitude of divine life to be mediated for us not by himself as the vine but by a different divine Person.

We have now distinguished three ways in which God appears in Judaeo-Christian thinking. He is the unique, solitary source of

[153]

everything else – a view that we take in admiring creation and respecting living organisms generally. He is a tribal god who herds us as a shepherd and gives us laws as a people or race. We think of him in this way to the extent to which we think we have duties to him, fear his judgements on us, feel that what he orders is good and what he forbids is bad, and desire to live as members of a divinely instituted community. And we think he has concern for us as individuals; we think this insofar as we act in order to receive his supernatural gifts as individuals and attain to the kind of supernatural life for which he destines us. These three ways of thinking of God correspond to our three ways of thinking of ourselves. We are material objects, parts of a physical world; we are social beings; and we are the objects of, and reciprocate, individual concern.

There can be no doubt that Christians do think of God in the three ways described. I hope it will be agreed too that these ways of thinking of God are similar to the ways in which we think of human beings when we think of them as egoists, as social beings and as altruists. But a human being is not three persons; a human being is surely one person that acts in three ways. Why should we say that God is three persons rather than a single person who created the universe, decided to enter into social relations with creatures, and acts within creatures? It is time to face the Sabellian charge.

Even when we are speaking of human beings, it is not quite accurate to say that it is the same person who acts in the three ways. If the trisection of the psyche I have been using is correct, we have strictly speaking three distinct notions of a person or intelligent, purposive agent. There are egoist agents, social agents and altruists, and we have no single generic concept of anything common to all three. All act for reasons and purposes, but their reasons and purposes are heterogeneous. Egoist, dutiful and altruistic acts are all understood teleologically, but there are still three varieties of teleological understanding. That being so, we can say that a person identified at one time or in one way is the same person as one identified at another, only if we can say it is the same

[154]

egoist, or the same social agent, or the same altruist. We can say, 'The artist who created that picture is the same egoist as the gourmet now enjoying that wine.' But we cannot say, 'It is the same person as the officer who risked his life to save the men in his platoon,' since it is neither the same egoist nor the same social being – unless it is as a social being and not just as solitary hedonist that the ex-officer is now enjoying the wine. Similarly we can say, 'The officer who saved the men under him was the same social being as the husband who was unfaithful to his wife,' but we cannot say, 'It was the same person as the bird-lover who looked after the raven with the broken wing,' unless it was not just out of duty but out of concern for the men under him as individuals that the officer risked his life for them. It is not that we cannot claim that the artist, the officer and the bird-lover are identical, but it is better to say that they are the same human being. For the concept of a human being is precisely the concept of a living organism that has these three modes of agency. If that is right, we cannot say that the person who created the universe is the same person as the one who decided to enter into society with creatures or even the one who makes the good of individuals his own objective. The most we can say is that it is the same God. And being the same God is very different from being the same human being.

That is because God, at least in the Judaeo-Christian tradition, has no body. A human being is an organism with sense-organs and limbs it learns to move as it wishes. Any action for which a human being is responsible is either action by those limbs themselves or else caused by movements of them. The gallant officer is the same human being as the wine-drinking painter and the bird-lover who cherishes the raven because the hands that drag the men to safety are the same as those that lift the wine glass and bandage the wing. Further, any action for which a human being is responsible must be for a reason correlated with a physical state of that organism's sensory system. We should not think Othello responsible for Desdemona's death if we did not think he moved his limbs for the reason that she loved Cassio; and we should not think his movements were for that reason if we did not think her loving Cassio was implied by words uttered by Iago that affected Othello's ears. But God is not supposed to have either limbs or sense-organs. I suggest that the role of the body in the identity of a human being is our ground for saying that a human being is rather a single thing with three aspects than a trinity. The body is what provides something for the aspects to be aspects of. Because God does not have a body, what in our dealings with a human being would be thinking of different aspects, in our dealings with him is thinking of different persons.

But if the body is what unifies the three aspects of a human being, and God is bodiless, what unifies the divine Persons? What stops them from being three Gods? Does not this circumnavigation of the Charybdis of Sabellianism expose us to the Scylla of tritheism?

Judaeo-Christian monotheism is founded on the belief that the universe depends on a single creator: light shines, rain falls and physical processes generally go on because that is the will of one God. The monotheist rejects the possibility that some processes should go on because one God so wishes, and others because another; and superhuman agents who, like the Olympian gods, are not creators, are not allowed to be genuine Gods at all. If the Son, therefore, were not the same God as the creator he would not be truly divine, and even if we could share in his life, that would not be sharing in divine life. The same goes for the Spirit: the gift of the Spirit can be a gift of divine life only if it is the same God that creates the world and that dwells in organisms. Tritheism is not a live option.

As I said at the beginning, the doctrine of the Trinity is best viewed, not on the model of a scientific theory as a description of God's nature, but as a formulation of the conception of God underlying Christian attitudes towards the natural world, the Church, religious practices and other people. We find that though Christians think there is only one God – they do not praise one creator for corn and another for doves and pigeons – God plays in their thought the three distinct roles that human beings do when they are thought of as egoists, as social beings and as altruists. But Christians cannot think just that God is one thing with three aspects as they think a human being is. For a human being is a living organism, whereas God is supposed to be bodiless. So it is best to say that Christians think that the divine nature subsists in three distinct Persons, or that there are three Persons in God.

NINE

Religious Truth

The excellent weather which greeted the Vevekukumis on their arrival at Windyhaugh continued throughout their stay. On the Sunday morning, after Miss Witherington and the Vevekukumis returned from church, the whole party went down to the river. A quarter of a mile below the house, it formed a good swimming pool. At the top end were rocks from which one could dive, at the bottom was a small sandy beach on which one could bask. Except for Mr Dodson, who seemed to dislike undressing, everyone did both things. They were accompanied by several bottles of wine in ingenious things to keep them cool, and wine glasses because Miss Witherington never drank wine out of anything else. By this time Sue as well as Charles had become friendly with the Vevekukumis, and as she and Ligea lay drying side by side in the sun she had no diffidence about asking rather a personal question.

Sue: Did you and Ernest go to church with Ursie?

Ligea: Yes. Don't you ever go to church, Sue?

Sue: Sometimes, when I'm in the country and everyone else goes. But I'm not very religious. Do you believe in God, and Jesus, and all that?

Ligea: Yes.

Sue: Does everyone in the Iles des Nuages?

Ligea: Yes.

Sue: Well, I suppose it's true for you.

[158]

Charles: I think it's nonsense to say that.

Ligea: Why? I think it's very sensible. For us, in the Iles des Nuages, it is true, and also for Cousin Ursie; but for most people in Europe it is not true.

Charles: All that means is that you and my aunt think it's true, and most people in Europe think it's false.

Ligea: But that is what I said, Charles.

Charles: No, you said it was true for some people, and was false for others. But a thing can't be both true and false.

Sue: Which do you think it is, then?

Charles: I don't know. I believe my mother was like Ursie, she thought it was true. But after she died we settled down into being rather an agnostic family. I think questions about God are rather like questions about other planets. You wouldn't say that there are people on other planets for you but not for me; it's just that I don't see how anyone can be sure whether there are people on other planets or not.

Mr Dodson: I don't think it's quite like that. I'm on the side of Ligea and Sue here. I think you have to distinguish two kinds of truth, what one might call 'literal' truth and 'profound' truth. Whether there are people on other planets is a question of literal truth, and you're right, Charles, either there are or there aren't. But when you talk about God and the soul and death you're talking about the deepest things in life, and your statements have a different kind of truth.

Charles: What kind is that?

Miss Witherington: I can tell you that. It comes in this book Eddie has lent me. [After her swim Miss Witherington had been lying with a book and a glass within earshot.] Shall I read it to you?

Charles: Please do.

Miss Witherington: It says that an utterance is 'profoundly true' if it has 'the capacity to enhance tremendously my life here and now, giving it an inner harmony and peace far beyond what material enjoyments, or even what the more sophisticated enjoyments afforded by the arts, can provide; and furthermore, to enable me

[159]

to lead a life that is morally better and more contributory to the good of those among whom I live than would otherwise be possible.'[1]

Sue: I think that's right. And what enhances one person's life and works for them, doesn't work for someone else. So religion is true for you, Ligea, but not for me. Is that what you mean, Eddie?

Mr Dodson: Yes.

Charles: What do you think, Ernest? Oh. He's gone back into the water. Well, what about you, Ligea? Does religion give you an inner harmony and peace beyond what material enjoyments can provide?

Ligea: No.

Charles: Who wrote this stuff?

Miss Witherington: Someone called Hugo Meynell. Eddie thought I'd be interested because I once knew him, but I don't see how I could have done.

Charles: But do you agree with what he says?

Miss Witherington: He doesn't really agree with it himself. He's putting up a target to shoot at, isn't that right, Eddie?

Sue: But religion does help religious people to lead better lives, doesn't it?

Miss Witherington: Not always. Sometimes it makes them cruel, or just smug.

Sue: Then it isn't really true for them. Not deep down, it isn't; it's only superficial.

Charles: I still can't understand this talk of being true for somebody. And apparently Professor Meynell doesn't either. Does anyone apart from Sue find it convincing?

Mr Dodson: Oh yes, it's quite an old idea. Not all utterances are intended to state facts. Some are intended to influence our conduct and actions by raising various pictures in our minds and various feelings. That is the purpose of religious language.

Charles: It must have been difficult for missionaries to the Iles des Nuages, where they didn't have pictures.

Ligea: M. Eddie doesn't mean that people have to think of pictures. He means people think of things the Europeans paint, like God touching Adam's hand and bringing him to life; but he believes that thinking of anything is having a picture of it in the mind.

Mr Dodson: How perceptive you are, Ligea.

Sue: Well, that's how the story of Adam and Eve works, isn't it? I mean, nobody thinks that God really did touch Adam's hand with his finger. Do you think that, Ligea?

Ligea: No.

Sue: Or that Eve really ate an apple? Though I don't know what that story is supposed to do for us.

Mr Dodson: Produce in us a lively sense of our unworthiness, according to Berkeley.[2]

Ligea: Who is Berkeley?

Mr Dodson: He was a bishop. And he also had an interpretation of the doctrine of the Trinity.

Ligea: Ah, that is a doctrine for a bishop, that.

Mr Dodson: Berkeley said that 'A man may believe the doctrine of the Trinity, provided that this doctrine of a creator, redeemer and sanctifier makes proper impressions on his mind, producing therein hope, gratitude and obedience, and thereby becomes a lively operating principle influencing his life and actions.'[3]

Ernest [emerging from the river]: You are all looking very serious. What are you talking about?

Ligea: M. Eddie is explaining to us the mystery of the Holy Trinity.

Ernest: M. Eddie can explain anything: he is a philosopher. Dear Cousin, may I have a glass of wine? You have a large trout in this pool. Would you like me to catch it?

Charles: You think because you have been to church you can forget about religion for the rest of the day. But we're having our service now. M. Eddie says there are two kinds of truth. If you say there's a big trout in the pool, that's true if there's a big trout in the pool – weighing more than a kilogram, say?

Ernest: Two kilograms, at least.

Miss Witherington: What a wonderful fish. Don't disturb it, Ernest. I feel the pool belongs to it as much as to me.

Charles: And false if there isn't. But if someone says God exists, that's true if it gives his life an inner harmony and makes him nice to other people, and false if it doesn't. Have I got it right?

Mr Dodson: That's more or less the position Meynell was explaining, and it has the backing of weighty authorities.

Ligea: Mgr Berkeley?

Mr Dodson: And Wittgenstein.

Ligea: Another bishop?

Mr Dodson: No, a philosopher.

Sue [to Miss Witherington]: But this other philosopher that you're reading objects to it?

Miss Witherington: So far as I can make out, he thinks when we say that there are three Persons in God or that Christ rose from the dead, we are trying to state facts, and our statements are true or false in the ordinary way.

Ernest: And that is the profound truth, that there are three Persons, but only one God.

Miss Witherington: No, that's the superficial truth. The profound truth is to be nice, happy people.

Ernest: I'm afraid I did not understand. I speak English very badly.

Charles: But does Meynell merely assert that religious utterances are meant to state facts? Because the other side, presumably, will say this is just a misunderstanding. Or has he any argument?

Miss Witherington: I'm not sure. I haven't read the book carefully enough.

Mr Dodson: Can you think of any argument? You started by being rather scornful of this notion of profound truth.

Charles: Ligea, Eddie is challenging me. I can't answer without your help. Don't go to sleep on us.

Ligea: I am not going to sleep. I thought I would have another swim before lunch; and I want to see the big trout.

Charles: Can you help me against Eddie's theory? He says that language has two purposes . . .

[162]

Ligea: Yes, I heard what he said. One purpose is to state facts, to say things, the other is to influence people. But everyone who speaks has both purposes. I do not speak to you at all unless I want you to think something or to do something. But I want to influence you by what I say, and I count on your knowing what that is. To understand me you must know both my purposes, *ce que je veux dire et ce que je veux faire*. When Mgr Berkeley talks about God, what he wants to do is to excite images of things in us, or give us comfort or fortitude. If he finds the right words for this, his sermon is useful, eloquent, like those of Boissier. But what he wants to say and what he wants to do, they are not alternative significations like the significations of the *calembours* the English like. And to call a useful utterance 'true' or a useless one 'false', that is just to abuse the words 'true' and 'false'. Those words regard what is said, not its practical utility. I speak truly, not if you do what I want you to do, but if things are as I say they are.

Mr Dodson: And if they aren't as you say they aren't? We know your fondness for denials, Ligea.

Charles: They keep your polar bears away. So we are saying, Ligea, that there is only one way of being true, and it is the same whether we are talking about God, or numbers, or history, or physics?

Ligea: Perhaps. But God is different from numbers and atoms and the forces of physics. Perhaps when the things we talk about are different, how it is for them to be as we say is different.

Charles: How do you mean?

Ligea: You remember on Thursday, when M. Eddie asked us about truth, we gave him a simple answer? If I say that this wine is white, I speak truly because the wine is the colour I say it is. And if I say that Sue is not between you and me I speak falsely, because the order in which we are lying is the order in which I deny we are lying. But when we speak about God, truth is not an affair of colours or positions.

Mr Dodson: What is it an affair of, then?

Miss Witherington: I certainly understand that utterance, Eddie:

you want us to stay here talking about truth. But I think Ligea is right, and we should have another swim.

[Everyone entered the water except Mr Dodson, who had found himself a comfortable seat on the shelving rocks, and thought that the swimmers looked very charming from there. Ernest located the large trout and Miss Witherington gave strict orders it was not to be harassed. Having got themselves into a good state to enjoy the sun and more wine, they returned and Ernest and Charles disposed themselves on either side of Mr Dodson, while Miss Witherington, Sue and Ligea stretched out on the sand. The two groups were within speaking distance of one another.]

Mr Dodson [to Ernest]: This is how I imagine the Iles des Nuages. Is it really like this?

Ernest: We have more clouds, and the bushes are greener and thicker. But yes, though sometimes it rains, often it is like this.

Mr Dodson: No wonder you believe in God. It must be like living in heaven.

Charles: Do you think it is easier to believe in God if life is good? I think people are more religious when things seem desperate.

Mr Dodson: Because the thought of God gives them hope?

Charles: I suppose so.

Mr Dodson: Then I suspect that though you don't realise it, you agree with Wittgenstein. He says 'There's this extraordinary use of the word "believe". People talk of believing, but they don't use "believe" as one does ordinarily . . . If the question arises as to the existence of God, it plays an entirely different role from that of the existence of any person or object I've ever heard of.'[4]

Charles: Wittgenstein thinks saying 'I believe God exists' is like having a sort of charm you hold on to when you're anxious or depressed?

Mr Dodson: Don't you?

Charles: Do you hear that, Ligea?

Ligea: Yes.

Charles: Do you agree with Mgr Wittgenstein?

[164]

Ligea: He is not a bishop, so I do not have to agree with him.

Mr Dodson: But do you really think that believing God exists is like believing that you exist, or that air or water exists?

Ligea: Perhaps. What is it like to believe that I exist?

Mr Dodson: I see and hear you.

Ligea: Do you see and hear me existing? We do not have a word like 'exist' in Eoenanian. In French or English you say 'Ligea believes God exists,' or 'Charles believes the water in that pool exists.' We would not say that in Eoenanian, and I think when you say it, you do not tell us anything we believe, you merely tell us what our beliefs are about.

Charles: I don't quite follow that, Ligea. What do you mean?

Ligea: You see the pool and you think, 'The water is deep, there,' or perhaps you wonder, 'Is the water cold?' Either way, M. Eddie, who is a philosopher, would say you think the water exists. It is just a European way of saying that it comes into your thoughts. It does not tell us what the thoughts are.

Mr Dodson: So when I say that in the Iles des Nuages people believe that God exists, I merely say that God comes into their thoughts, and not what their thoughts are.

Ligea: You do not say what the thoughts are. But when I say, 'M. Eddie knows I exist,' I mean not just that I come into your thoughts, but that you think I am a person, and when you say we believe God exists you mean we think he is a person [*une personne*].

Mr Dodson: So that is the thought he comes into, that he is a person? You have a word for a person?

Ligea [laughing]: You keep thinking we are philosophers. We have a word '*enana*', but it is not quite like your word 'person' when you say, 'In the Iles des Nuages they think God is a person.' We should never say, 'We think God is *enana*.'

Mr Dodson: What do you believe about God, then?

Ligea: What do you believe about me? Perhaps you think, 'If I speak to her, she will reply.'

Mr Dodson: I think, 'If I throw a stone into that pool, I shall hear

[165]

a splash and see a ripple.' Do I think the water is a person?

Ligea: Only if you think it splashes in order to reply, and the wave moves in order to wet the rocks. Then an anthropologist will say: 'Look! M. Eddie is an animist. He thinks the water is a person.'

Mr Dodson: All right. You think it is true to say, ' I think Ligea is a person,' or, 'I think you exist', because I think you do things for reasons and purposes?

Ligea: Yes, and that is not like thinking that I am brown or that if you push me in the pool there will be a splash. That is why I said that beliefs about God are not true like beliefs about colours or physics. When God comes into our thoughts, it is as a person.

Mr Dodson: But you do not see God go swimming, or hear him speak.

Ligea: No, but we see and hear the river. In the Iles des Nuages we believe that the wind blows and the rain falls and the rivers run because that is what God wants, just as when I swim my arms and legs move because that is what I want. We think God made the world on purpose, for us and for the other creatures in it, like that large trout.

Sue: Do you believe what it says in the Bible, about God making the world in seven days, just by magic?

Miss Witherington: I don't know about Ligea, but I don't think of creation as a sort of rival theory to what scientists say about the origin of the universe.

Mr Dodson: No. You think of it as a colourful myth.

Miss Witherington: Thank you, Eddie, but I don't think it a myth either. The scientists are trying to tell us what processes go on in the universe, and what came out of what and how. But if you believe God created the universe you believe that these processes started, and still go on now, because that is what God wants. It's not just luck that we're here; the natural order that produced us exists because God wants us to be here.

Mr Dodson: That's what you say, Ursie, but what does it really amount to? Isn't it just a way of saying that you think the world is pretty nice?

[166]

Miss Witherington: Well, I do think it's a good world, and perhaps that's partly why I go to church, to thank God for it. But believing God made it for the benefit of his creatures ought to stop us from destroying it the way we do, and make us treat animals with respect – though I can't say I'm a terribly green person.

Mr Dodson: I'm sure you're as green as your neighbours. But let's leave the existence of God for a moment, and consider some other religious beliefs. I trust that in the Iles des Nuages they believe there are three persons in God?

Ligea: Of course.

Mr Dodson: Have I succeeded in saying something you believe about God, or only made another philosophical comment on unstated beliefs?

Ligea: Am I a philosopher? You will have to tell me. I think M. Eddie believes there are three persons on this sand?

Mr Dodson: Three very charming persons.

Miss Witherington: You have no idea, Eddie, how elderly you sound when you try to be gallant.

Ligea: Is that something you believe about us, that there are three persons here?

Sue: It's just believing we exist, isn't it?

Mr Dodson: I don't think it's quite the same. Ligea says one can't say in Eoenenian 'Ligea, Sue and Ursie exist,'; but I feel sure you can say, 'There are three women on the beach.'

Ligea: Ernest often says things like that – or thinks them.

Mr Dodson: So it is not a philosopher's comment. But it says nothing about purposes.

Sue: I still don't see that it says anything at all except that we exist.

Miss Witherington: It's saying there are three of us, that we're three different women.

Ligea: Yes, and when you say, 'M. Eddie thinks we are three different women,' you are not telling us anything he believes about any of us.

Mr Dodson: Certainly it is not something I believe about Ligea Vevekukumi that she is three different women; but cannot it be

[167]

something I believe about all three of you, that you are three different women?

Ligea: What is this thing that you believe about all of us when you believe we are three different women?

Mr Dodson: Perhaps I think there are just as many of you as there are glasses on the sand, or natural numbers between 0 and 4.

Miss Witherington: What on earth are you talking about, Eddie? That can't be what you mean when you say that Sue, Ligea and I are three different people.

Charles: You know that Ligea is between Sue and Aunt Ursie. If you know that, doesn't it follow that you know they are three different people?

Ligea: Certainly that is a thought about three people, not just one or two. Saying that he thinks we are three tells us that, not what his thought about the three of us is.

Mr Dodson: But surely you don't want to say the same about the Christian belief that there are three persons in God – that Christians believe that the Son is between the Father and the Holy Ghost?

Ligea: No. Only that when you say we believe there are three Persons in God you are not stating one of our beliefs; you are saying that certain beliefs we hold that you have not stated are beliefs about different persons.

Mr Dodson: What beliefs are they? Not about spatial relations, evidently.

Ligea: The beliefs that Mgr Berkeley spoke of: that God the Father created the world, God the Son became a man and died for us, and the Holy Spirit comes to us in the sacraments and sanctifies us.

Charles: Are you saying that philosophers came along and examined these beliefs, and concluded that Christians think that the Father, Son and Holy Ghost are three different persons but only one God?

Miss Witherington: You make it sound implausible, but that's really what happened in the first four or five centuries AD, except that

[168]

it was theologians rather than philosophers.

Mr Dodson: And they stated their conclusions as dogmas.

Ligea: Europeans like to state everything as dogma. But the real Christian beliefs are about the creation, and the life of Our Lord, and the Church and the Sacraments. And those are all beliefs about God's purposes, about why he created the world, about why his Son came into the world, about what he wants us to do in the world . . .

Charles: And not do. There's a lot of that.

Mr Dodson: Not all beliefs about God are like that, though. Don't you believe that God knows everything?

Ligea: Yes, we are told that.

Mr Dodson [consulting his diary]: Well, it's full moon tonight. Does God know that?

Charles: When Christians say God knows everything, they don't mean that he knows the location of every physical body at every moment relatively to every inertial frame.

Mr Dodson: Why not? That's what I should mean. You see how words mean something different in religious talk and to ordinary people.

Ligea: You are an ordinary person, M Eddie?

Mr Dodson: As ordinary as they come.

Ligea: And you know that the moon will be full tonight. What makes it true that you know that?

Mr Dodson: What makes it true that it will be full moon?

Ligea: No, what makes it true that you have this belief that it will be full?

Mr Dodson: I suppose I have a sort of picture of a full moon . . . '

[General outcry. Shouts of, 'You're not allowed to talk about pictures to people from the Iles des Nuages.']

Mr Dodson [a little huffily]: Well, you tell me what makes it true.

Ligea: If, after dinner tonight, you were to say, 'Let's go out and look at the moon,' and you said this because the moon is full, or because your diary says so, then you must believe that the moon is full.

[169]

Mr Dodson: If I act for the reason that it's full, yes.

Ligea: And it would be a kind thing for you to do? Because we should all enjoy looking at the full moon.

Mr Dodson: Yes.

Ligea: Perhaps God wants you to do this kind thing. Perhaps because the moon is full he wants you to suggest that we all go out.

Mr Dodson: If God exists, and cares about you and me, I dare say he wants that.

Ligea: And if he wants it, he acts in order that it may come about?

Mr Dodson: Acts how? Keeps me going? Keeps the solar system going?

Ligea: For that purpose, among others.

Mr Dodson: If God is now keeping the moon in its course partly in order that I, Edward Dodson, may propose a moon-gazing excursion after dinner, then, dear Ligea, unless he wants to disappoint us all, God must know that the moon is full.

Ligea: And he no more needs a picture than you. [General applause]

Sue: Ligea met your challenge there, didn't she, Eddie?'

Ligea: Only with M. Eddie's help. He is very chivalrous. It is not true, what Cousin Ursie says about his gallantry.

Mr Dodson: But what about life after death? How does belief in that fit with your ideas of religious belief?

Ligea: In the Iles des Nuages you see us pray for the dead. So you say, 'They believe the dead exist.' If they did not exist, our prayers would not help them.

Mr Dodson: I'm not sure that I see how they could help them, even if they do exist.

Ligea: Because they are dead? Or do you not see how prayers could help people even when they are not dead?

Mr Dodson: That too, I'm afraid.

Ligea: And we pray *to* the dead as well as *for* them, we ask them to help us. Cousin Ursie thinks my grandmother helped Andromache, my sister, to find a good husband. You will say that if she thinks that, she believes my grandmother exists, though she is dead.

Mr Dodson: Do you really believe that, Ursie? That God worked a miracle to find your cousin a husband?

Ligea [laughing]: It did not need a miracle.

Mr Dodson: But then how was it an answer to prayer?

Miss Witherington: You don't always pray for miracles, Eddie. Sometimes you pray that people will be sensible.

Mr Dodson: But isn't that asking God to work a miracle to make them sensible?

Miss Witherington: Why this passion for the miraculous? What do you mean by a 'miracle'?

Mr Dodson: 'A transgression of a law of nature by a particular volition of the Deity.'[5]

Miss Witherington: What does that mean?

Mr Dodson: Something that happens contrary to the laws of nature because God says, 'Let it happen.'

Miss Witherington: But what has that to do with behaving sensibly?

Mr Dodson: I suppose you agree that how we behave depends on what goes on in our brains, what neurons fire and so forth. If God is going to make someone behave sensibly he'll have to interfere with the electrical processes in that person's cerebral cortex.

Miss Witherington: Really, Eddie, you make God sound like the man who comes out to mend the computer when it breaks down. If somebody one loved had Alzheimer's and their neurones were packing up altogether perhaps one might pray for a miracle in your sense. But when it's a matter of two people seeing the good points in each other, surely the laws of nature are neither here nor there.

Mr Dodson: We're touching here on a big subject. But anyhow the belief that there is a life after death is the belief that the dead help us and can be helped?

Miss Witherington: I suppose it also shows in our acting in the hope that after death we shall be with God.

[171]

Mr Dodson: That's more a belief about the future, that you *will* exist after death, than a belief about the present. It's a tricky question whether beliefs about the future can be true or false now. But the other beliefs we've been talking about, if you and Ligea are right, definitely are true or false now? And they are true if things are as you think they are, and false if they aren't?

Ligea: Yes, and they differ from beliefs about stones you throw into the river in that they are all about reasons and purposes, so that they are true if things really do happen in order to benefit us and God really has the purposes we think, and they are false if God's purposes are not what we think, or things happen for no reason or purpose at all.

Miss Witherington: I think we should have something to eat while Eddie is pondering that, and put a complete ban on the supernatural until after lunch. Then, if he likes, Eddie can demolish our religious beliefs while we are digesting our food before swimming again.

[This plan was immediately agreed to. The swimmers wrapped themselves in Polynesian *pareus*, which made a sufficiently formal costume, and a large, vacuum-lined chest was opened to reveal crab mayonnaise, salad, ice cream, cake, fruit and a fresh supply of wine. The embargo on supernatural topics was scrupulously maintained until the end of the ice cream, but Sue had placed herself next to Mr Dodson, and as she peeled her peach she fixed him with slightly mischievous eyes and asked whether he had agreed with what Ligea had said. Mr Dodson would usually, after such a lunch and on such a day, have been inclined to a nap. But the figure of Sue, clad only in her *pareu*, so close to him militated against sleep, and it was an adamantine rule with him never to decline an opening to give a tutorial. 'How do you mean?' he asked a little weakly.]

Sue: Well, if she's right about religious beliefs, they're true or false literally, and not just in the deep way. I mean, it's true literally, isn't it, that we came here because there's this pool and in order to swim? Only you didn't come to swim, so perhaps it isn't true for you.

[172]

Mr Dodson: I don't think that making the universe is quite on a par with walking a quarter of a mile, or driving á landrover like you and Ursie. But in any case, most philosophers would say that any explanation in terms of reasons and purposes can be rephrased in other terms. They don't think that reasons and purposes really enter into the content of our beliefs at all. We can believe, as Ligea says, that this wine is red or that that boulder is five feet from us, but we don't really believe that things happen for reasons or purposes.

Sue: Why not?

Charles: I can tell you why. It's because of those pictures that Eddie isn't supposed to mention. Philosophers think that the thought of anything is like a mirror image of it. They conceive the mind as the mirror of nature.

Sue: Yes, Julian had a book called that.[6] But it wasn't as interesting as the title.

Charles: It wouldn't be. But philosophers think that if my beliefs are true, my mind is like a mirror that is perfectly smooth and flat, and reflects things with perfect accuracy. If my beliefs are false, my mind is like a distorting mirror. The belief that there's a glass of wine beside me when there isn't, is like an image of a glass of wine that spookily appears in a mirror when there is no glass in front of it. But there's no more to an image of me knocking a glass over on purpose than there is to an image of me just knocking over a glass. So purposiveness doesn't enter into beliefs.

Sue: That's rather a good theory, Charles, I can understand that. Is that what you meant, Eddie?

Mr Dodson: Not exactly. The theory won't quite do as it stands. Because what about the belief that there isn't a glass of wine beside you?

Sue: That would be like a picture of Charles with nothing beside him.

Mr Dodson: Well, what about the belief that there isn't a large pink frog beside Charles? That's quite different from the belief that

[173]

there isn't a glass; so they can't both be like a picture of him with nothing beside him.

Sue: But you can tinker with the theory a bit, and make it better?

Mr Dodson: Yes. You can't have a picture of Charles not having a glass beside him; you can only have a picture of him having one. But we can say that the belief that he doesn't have a glass is true if a picture of him with a glass is false. Do you ever read detective stories?

Sue: I've watched Inspector Morse on the telly.

Mr Dodson: Well, suppose that the Master of the college is murdered in the college chapel, and the Bursar says that at the time he was reading in the Bodleian. Inspector Morse believes that if the Bursar was in the Bodleian, he didn't commit the murder. Now you can't have a picture of someone not committing a murder if he's in the Bodleian. But you can have a picture of the Bursar reading in the Bodleian and another picture of him committing the murder in the chapel. You can then say that this belief of the Inspector, the belief that if the Bursar was in the Bodleian he didn't commit the murder, is true unless the two pictures of him beavering in Bodley and butchering in the chapel are both true.

Sue [trying to puzzle it out]: Both true? Both false, you mean?

Charles: We haven't just got pictures here, we've got polar bears. These are pictures which are true or false in themselves, and Ligea and I don't believe in such things at all.

Mr Dodson: You needn't have polar bears if you don't want them. You can say that the Inspector's belief is true unless it's true of the Bursar both that he's in Bodley and that he's in the college chapel. So you're explaining the truth or falsity of the Inspector's complex belief in terms of the Bursar's being related or not being related in a certain way to each of the two buildings. But now consider the sort of thing Ligea wants to say: 'The Bursar killed the Master for the reason that the Master had seduced his wife.' That might be true whether or not the Master seduced the wife, and false whether or not the Bursar killed him. So its truth

[174]

can't be explained in terms of its being true or false of the Master that he did the seduction, and its being true or false of the Bursar that he did the murder.

Sue: Ligea's asleep. It isn't fair to criticise her theory when she can't defend it.

Charles: I'll defend it for her. According to you, we ought to be able to say what it is for a belief to be true in terms of things having or not having properties, or standing or not standing in relations.

Mr Dodson: Yes.

Charles: But before lunch you were talking about throwing a stone that causes a ripple in the pool. You think that the water ripples because the stone falls in. But the truth of that can't be explained in terms of its being true of the stone that it falls in the water, and true of the water that it ripples. Something else might make it ripple, Ernest's big trout rising, for example.

Mr Dodson: Very well, perhaps besides the idea of having a property we shall need the idea of causal relations. In fact that is what I'd use in the college murder case. I'd say that the Bursar was caused to kill the Master by a mental picture of the Master making love to his wife. But once we've got things having and not having properties, and events causing and not causing other events, that's enough. Let's draw the line there, and not burden ourselves with reasons and purposes as well. Conceptual economy should be our watchword.

Charles: Thrift is a virtue, miserliness is a vice. I notice academics are quick enough to complain when the government cuts their grants. Religionists can ask for more than vague talk about economy to justify slashing their conceptual resources in this way.

Mr Dodson: Perhaps they're not genuine resources. Perhaps they're just fairy gold.

Miss Witherington [rousing herself from a doze]: You seem to be having rather an intense conversation over there.

Sue: Eddie was attacking what Ligea said before lunch, and Charles was defending it.

[175]

Miss Witherington: Ligea is pretty good at defending herself.

Sue: She and Ernest are asleep.

Ernest [stirring and sitting up]: We are not asleep any more. We heard you talking but your voices sounded so pleasant we did not like to intervene.

Sue: Charles defended you very well, Ligea, didn't he? He can be quite clever when he tries.

Ligea: Charles is always brilliant. But what did he say?

Sue: Eddie tried to prove that we don't really believe anything happens for the sake of anything. But Charles said the same argument would prove that we can't believe anything causes anything else, which we obviously do. So it's perfectly possible to think that everything happens in order to fulfil God's will, though of course it doesn't follow anything really does. That's where faith comes in.

Ligea: Ah yes. But M. Eddie, why can we not really think that anything is ever done for anyone or for any purpose? Everyone thinks that.

Charles: It's that theory of his that you mentioned yourself this morning. He believes that something can come into our thought only if there can be a picture of it, and there cannot be a picture of something's being *for* something.

Ligea: Perhaps he is right about that, but it does not matter.

Charles: What do you mean?

Ligea: I am still asleep. I am going to have a swim now, and then I shall be able to think clearly. Come on, Sue, let us see if Ernest's trout is having lunch.

[Ligea and Sue went into the pool, followed by everyone except Mr Dodson. When they emerged Ligea's eyes were as sparkling as the water. She called for her *pareu* and knotting it under her arms, squatted down on the sand. Everyone gathered round expectantly. Mr Dodson showed some uneasiness at the proximity involved but Sue and Miss Witherington hemmed him in on either side like a prisoner between two policemen.]

Ligea: Now, M. Eddie, you think that Polynesians do not know what pictures are. I am going to show you how we picture some things, and think others without picturing them. [Draws on the sand] What is that?

Mr Dodson: It looks like a fish.

Ligea: It is Ernest's big trout. Now I draw a spear, and Ernest swimming. Because there is a trout, in order to spear it, Ernest swims.

Miss Witherington: I hope not.

Ligea: But M. Eddie agrees that if that is so, Ernest knows there is a trout. But all that comes into his thought is the trout. [Draws a frame round the fish.] There, the trout is in a picture-frame. Now I add Cousin Ursie shouting 'Don't kill it!' [Draws a face with an open mouth.]

Mr Dodson: I see. The trout's being Ernest's reason for swimming is her reason for shouting. So she knows that Ernest sees the trout. But then the fact that his swimming is for that reason ought to come into her picture. You should draw a frame round the fish, the spear and the swimming. [Does so.]

Ligea: No. Her reason is only that there is a trout. But to stop Ernest from spearing it she shouts. And if she shouts for that purpose, she thinks Ernest knows there is a trout. [Rubs out Mr Dodson's frame, puts back the frame round the fish, and draws a line under the spear.]

Mr Dodson: What does that line mean?

Ligea: Ernest's spearing the trout is what she shouts to prevent.

Charles: I do not think you would be so tender-hearted, Ligea. If you were swimming and saw the trout, you would stop in case, by going on, you frightened it away and spoilt Ernest's hunting.

Ligea [Rubbing out the line under the spear, and replacing the shouting face by a woman swimming with a line under it]: Yes, in order that Ernest may spear the trout, I refrain from swimming. But I still know that Ernest sees the trout, and my reason is simply that there is a trout. Seeing the trout, I am careful not to spoil Ernest's hunting. Of course I see him too – he is big enough.

[177]

Miss Witherington: Yes, Ligea, but you said God made the world for the benefit of the creatures in it, including the fish. Perhaps God does not want Ernest to kill the fish.

Ernest: *Le bon Dieu* will not blame us for killing fish if we are hungry.

Miss Witherington: What if you are not hungry? Then I think God might want you to leave it alone. How do you show that, Ligea, in your pictures?

Ligea: Let me see. If Ernest wants to spear the trout, he swims after it. [Drawing a trout, a spear and a man swimming.]

Miss Witherington: Yes.

Ligea: If you want him not to kill it, to stop him swimming, for fear that he spears it, you shout 'Stop.' The trout is framed as your reason, and the spear and Ernest swimming have a line under them, and you shout.

Ernest: And then I stop. If Cousin Ursie tells me not to do something, I do not do it.

Ligea: So we have shown what is in your thought when you stop for that reason.

Charles: But the question was what is in his mind when he thinks God wants him to stop.

Sue: I suppose he thinks God made the trout.

Mr Dodson: But surely he thinks God made all living things, including wasps and nettles. Does God want us not to kill anything? That goes beyond Buddhism, let alone Christianity.

Ligea: If Ernest thinks God wants him to have pity on the trout, he thinks God gives it its great, heavy body and its big sharp teeth to catch little trout, yes; but God also gives Ernest intelligence and health and other things to eat, in order that he will think mercifully of the trout. And perhaps he gives Cousin Ursie eyes to see what is happening and a voice to call out. If Ernest thinks that God wants him not to spear the trout, many things like that will come into his thought where before there was only the shouting and the spearing.

Ernest: I think that *le bon Dieu* gives me eyes and hands to hunt for

[178]

fish for Ligea. She does not mind eating them.

Charles: Yes, but I think her point is that teeth and eyes come into your picture, Ernest, but this relation of one thing being for another does not.

Ligea: No. And neither does God himself. You cannot draw him.

Mr Dodson: So according to you, the belief that God made the world is true if nature produces teeth in trout for the benefit of the trout, and voices in people to tell other people how to behave, and you have that belief if seeing the teeth and hearing the voice, you want to act in a certain way.

Ligea: Yes.

Mr Dodson: Obediently to the speaker, kindly to the trout and so on?

Ligea: Yes.

Mr Dodson: But then holding religious beliefs is a matter of having a certain attitude towards other people and animals.

Ligea: Of course.

Mr Dodson: But doesn't that deprive them of any objective truth?

Ligea: No more than beliefs about you, or Ernest or Cousin Ursie.

Sue: The beliefs come out not true only if it's not because God wants them to that things happen. That's what we said before lunch, isn't it, Ligea?

Mr Dodson: It seems to me there's a big gap between what it is to hold these beliefs and what it is for them to be true. When Ernest believes there's a trout, the belief is true if there really is a trout in the pool, and he holds the belief, according to Ligea, if he swims because it's there, and according to me, if he's moved to swim by a picture of it. In that case, having the belief and the belief's being true are obviously connected. But with religious beliefs, you could drop the truth and just keep the edifying attitudes.

Miss Witherington: You could drop the truth about the trout, too, and just go swimming after something that isn't there, but in the Iles des Nuages that would be thought rather silly, wouldn't it, Ernest?

Ernest: You wouldn't believe what people do who come to us on yachts from America.

Charles: Wait a minute. You want to say, Eddie, that people can be caused to move by pictures.

Mr Dodson: Or something like pictures.

Charles: I'm not sure I like that theory of human movement. But at least you want to have beliefs of some kind about causes. Now isn't there just the same gap between what it is to hold a belief about a cause and the belief's being true?

Mr Dodson: How is that?

Charles: Ligea, could you draw us a piece of causal thinking?

Ligea: A picture of a picture making Ernest swim? That is too difficult.

Charles: Then take something easier. After lunch Aunt Ursie put the bottle of wine we hadn't finished back into the cooler. Why did you do that, Aunt Ursie.

Miss Witherington: Look what you've done, Eddie. First you teach Ligea to ask these moronic questions, and now Charles. All right, I'll play along and say what you want. I thought that because the sun was shining on it, it was getting warm.

Charles: Draw that, Ligea.

Ligea: But you know that I cannot. Here is the sun, and here is the bottle. And look, smoke is coming out of the bottle to show that it is warm. But you are right, Charles, I cannot draw the causing.

Charles [to Miss Witherington]: Did you want the wine to become warm?

Miss Witherington: No, dear Socrates, I did not.

Mr Dodson: What does it matter? She could still have thought the sun was making it warm, even if she was completely indifferent what temperature it became.

Charles: In that case she wouldn't have thought about it at all. No, she wants to keep it cool, so to prevent it from getting warm she puts it in the cooler.

Ligea [drawing]: Here is the cooler.

Charles: Now, if I understand Polynesian picture-language, we put a frame round the sun and a line under the bottle.

Sue: What does that mean?

Charles: Because the sun is shining, for fear that the wine should become warm, Aunt Ursie puts it in the cooler.

Sue: And if she does that, she thinks the sun is making the wine warm. Has Charles got it right, Ligea?

Ligea: Charles gets everything right.

Charles: So holding this causal belief is having a certain anxious attitude to the sun and the wine, but the belief is true if the sun really does make the wine warm.

Mr Dodson: I think there is some marvellous causal property in the water of that pool. To be a match for you I should have to baptise myself in it. But I shall stick to that wine that Ursie so rationally removed from the sun. Could you spare a glass, please, for a silenced but unconverted atheist?

Notes

Introduction
1. J. Pestieau (1984) *Guerre et paix sans état*, Montreal, Hexagon, end papers.
2. W. Charlton (1986) 'Greek philosophy and the concept of an academic discipline', *History of Political Thought* 6, pp. 47–61. See also: (1987) 'Aristotelian powers', *Phronesis* 32, pp. 277–98; (1995) 'Aristotle in search of principles', Third Rosamond Kent Sprague Lecuture in Ancient Philosophy; (1996) 'Platonic arguments', *Aristotelian Society*, Suppl. Vol. 70, pp. 201–8.
3. W. Charlton (1991) *The Analytic Ambition*, Oxford, Basil Blackwell, ch. 2–4. See also: (1983/4) 'Force, form and content in linguistic expression', *Aristotelian Society, Proceedings* 84, pp. 123–43; (1996) 'Platonic arguments', *Aristotelian Society*, Suppl. Vol. 70, pp. 195–200.
4. W. H. Mallock (1887) *The New Republic*, reprinted n.d., London, Michael Joseph.

Chapter Four: Mental States and Physicalism
1. L. Wittgenstein (1953) *Philosophical Investigations*, Oxford, Basil Blackwell, 1. 308.
2. Ibid., 1, p. 154.
3. D. Davidson (1982) *Essays on Actions and Events*, Oxford, Clarendon Press, p. 211. See also, D. Davidson (1985) *Essays on Actions and Events*, (eds) B. Vermazen and Merill B. Hintikka, Oxford, Clarendon Press, p. 246.
4. R. Rorty (1980) *Philosophy and the Mirror of Nature*, Oxford, Basil Blackwell, p. 17.

[182]

5. S. Kripke (1980) *Naming and Necessity*, Oxford, Basil Blackwell, pp. 146–7.
6. P. Churchland (1984) *Matter and Consciousness*, Cambridge, Ma., Bradford Books, p. 3.
7. P. Carruthers (1986) *Introducing Persons*, London, Routledge, pp. 10–13.
8. C. A. Peacocke, *Holistic Explanation* (1979) Oxford, Clarendon Press, pp. 134–6.
9. Kripke, op. cit., p. 146.
10. B. Russell (1921) *The Analysis of Mind*, London, Allen & Unwin, ch. 3 and 12.
11. I quote from G. Ryle (1954) *Dilemmas*, Cambridge, Cambridge University Press, p. 56.
12. Mill, *Essays on Some Unsettled Questions in Political Economy*, reprinted London 1877, p. 134.

Chapter Six: Biblical Concepts of the Supernatural

1. B. Malinowski (1926) 'Magic, science and religion' in *Science, Religion and Reality*, (ed.) J. Needham, London, Sheldon Press.
2. L. Ward (1903) *Pure Sociology*, New York, NY., Macmillan, p. 134.
3. E. Durkheim (1912) *The Elementary Forms of the Religious Life*, (tr) J. W. Swain, London, Allen & Unwin.
4. Malinowski, op. cit., p. 82.
5. C. Turnbull (1961/93) *The Forest People*, London, Pimilico.
6. W. J. Perry (1923) *The Children of the Sun*, New York, NY., Dutton, p. 186.
7. R. G. Collingwood (1938) *The Principles of Art*, Oxford, Clarendon Press, ch. 4.
8. Aristotle, *Nicomachean Ethics* 2. 1107a33–1108a9; *Eudemian Ethics* 2. 1220b38–1221a12.

Chapter Seven: Philosophy and the Supernatural

1. C. McGinn (1989) 'Can we solve the mind-body problem?', *Mind* 98, pp. 353, 363, n. 18.
2. D. C. Dennett (1969) *Content and Consciousness*, London, Routledge and Kegan Paul, p. 5 .
3. D. C. Dennett (1984) *Elbow Room*, Boston, Ma., MIT Press, p. 28.
4. D. Davidson (1982) *Essays on Action and Events*, Oxford, Clarendon

Press, p. 47.

5. See J. Bennett (1976) *Linguistic Behaviour*, Cambridge, Cambridge University Press, ch. 2; and, D. Papineau (1991) 'Teleology and mental states', *Aristotelian Society*, Suppl. Vol. 65. Bennett develops the point that an organism, like a homing missile, might be so constructed that circumstances which make it necessary for it to move or change in a ceratin way if a certain outcome is to be realised, actually cause it to move or change in that way. Papineau adds the idea that something may be said to exist *for the sake of* a certain function if it was naturally selected because it discharged that function.

6. Dennett (1969), op. cit., p. 78.

7. R. Swinburne (1986) *The Evolution of the Soul*, Oxford, Clarendon Press.

8. Carruthers, op. cit., p. 64.

9. T. Penelhum (1970) *Survival and Disembodied Existence*, London, Routledge, ch. 5–6.

10. Leibniz, *Monadology*, etc. 'Monads' are non-material, mind-like entities, and in Leibniz' system, the only things that really exist.

Chapter Eight: The Trinity and the Tripartite Soul

1. W. Charlton (1996) 'Trisecting the Psyche', *Philosophical Writings* 1.

2. W. Charlton (1988) *Philosophy and Christian Belief*, London, Sheed & Ward, ch. 8.

3. 'Strong in their own resources, needing nothing from us, neither won by merit nor touched by anger.' *Lucretius* 1. 48–9.

4. Similarly, Ezek 37.14; cf. Wis 15.11. And see also Wis 11.24–6, the third notion cited earlier, which ends 'for your breath is in everything.'

Chapter Nine: Religious Truth

1. H. Meynell (1994) *Is Christianity True?*, London, Geoffrey Chapman, p. 38.

2. Berkeley, *Alciphron* 7.7–11.

3. Ibid.

4. L. Wittgenstein (1966) *Lectures on Aesthetics, Psychology and Religious Belief*, Oxford, Basil Blackwell, p. 59.

5. Hume, *Enquiry concerning Human Understanding*, s. 10 n. 3.

6. Rorty, op. cit.